I-POWER is the only way to run a business

I-POWER keeps me growing and growing

I-POWER builds vendor relationships

I-POWER made art so efficient...it's a miracle

I-POWER improves our statistical analysis every day

I-POWER makes me very versatile

I-POWER cut our turnover to near zero

I-POWER helped me change from artist to editor

I-POWER adds many skills to my receptionist job

I POWER

There's a new system to run a business –"I" Power.

"I" Power works....it's simple.... it's proven.

"I" Power makes money in tough times—and good times too.

Key: It cuts costs–increases sales—decrease turnover–*and makes change easy.*

"I" Power was designed far all business—big and small.

It works for non-profits too.

And–it will work for government. Widely applied, it can rebuild America.

It will show you how to develop great business even in bad times.

"I" Power principles are not difficult to adopt. They can be put to work quickly. It's results are amazing. Everyone can use "I" Power—those at the top and those at the bottom and those in between.

Have you ever asked yourself, "How can I make our company more productive? More competitive?"

Or: "How do I improve the morale of my employees in these tough times?"

This book clearly shows you how to fire up your staff and bring continuous improvement to your organization.

"I" Power was created by Martin Edelston, founder and owner of the giant publishing conglomerate, Boardroom, Inc. This is the company that gave America *The Book of Inside Information,* which has sold more than 2 million copies and *The Book of Secrets*—which has sold more than 500,000 copies.

"I" Power will teach you how to bring quality and continuing growth to the business that you're involved with, too.

It incorporates those positive approaches that are contained in the "I" words from which it takes its name: Ideas...impact ...improvement...incentive...increase...innovate...inspiration...integrity...intelligence...invention...etc.

"I" Power can easily be the most important book you have ever read!

Martin Edelston
Founder, President,
Boardroom, Inc.
publisher of
Bottom Line/Business,
Bottom Line/Health,
Bottom Line/Personal,
Moneysworth, and
Tax Hotline

Marion Buhagiar
Economist,
Time/ reporter,
*Fortune/*writer/editor
Time Life Books/editor
Boardroom Reports/
editor...and Founder
of Expert Connections

"I" Power

Published by the Greenwich Institute for American Education
55 Railroad Avenue, Greenwich, Connecticut 06830

Library of Congress Cataloging-in-Publication Data

"I" Power: The Secrets of Great Business in Bad Times / Martin Edelston and
Marion Buhagiar

1. United States—Economic conditions. 2. United States—Industries.
3. Employee motivation—United States. 4. Competition, International. I. Buhagiar,
Marion. II. Title.

HC106.8.E26   1992   658.4'02—dc20   92-22604
ISBN 0-88723-175-6

Printed in the United States of America

"I" Power

THE SECRETS OF GREAT BUSINESS IN BAD TIMES

Contents "I" Power Contents

The Authors

Marion Buhagiar

Marion Buhagiar began her career as an economist with the US Department of Commerce. She has been a business and financial writer for 35 years.

In the last two years she has been traveling around the country interviewing managers and workers in US companies where continuous improvement programs are being implemented.

Before she joined Boardroom, Inc. to start Boardroom Books, Marion had been a business reporter for *Time* magazine, a writer and editor for *Fortune* and an editor at Time-Life Books.

She now heads her own business writing firm, Expert Connections, in New York City and is a regular contributor to Boardroom's publications.

Martin Edelston

Martin Edelston founded Boardroom, Inc. in 1972, at the age of 43, after holding many jobs with large and small companies. He has worked since he was ten years old—delivering milk—and then as a dishwasher, lifeguard, advertising salesman, book club manager, circulation director and business manager.

Martin is the owner, chief executive and top editor of the publications of Boardroom, Inc., headquartered in Greenwich, Connecticut.

Boardroom publishes several national periodicals— *Bottom Line/Personal, Bottom Line/Business, Tax Hotline, Bottom Line/Tomorrow, Moneysworth* and *Bottom Line/Health*. Boardroom Books is one of the nation's largest publishers of nonfiction books.

I have seen the enemy…and he is us.
                                    —*Pogo*
                                    by Walt Kelly

Start Here

This is a book for people in business, government and nonprofit organizations who know that they don't have time to wait for the federal government's economic restructuring, new tax policies or government programs and initiatives to make their companies more productive and competitive.

"I" Power is for people in both large and small organizations.

It's for people who are seriously interested in effective operations…for heads of organizations…for heads of departments…for heads of teams or units…for individual workers.

"I" Power is for everyone who feels that work can be an opportunity for each of us to operate at our highest level…*if we work within an intelligent system.*

It's *not* another book about operating lean and mean. Not about downsizing or "rightsizing." Nor is it another sermon about how people are your company's most important resource.

Quite simply, the practical system described in this book—and proven in practice for several years now—shows the way to encourage every worker in the organization to *think*—think about the way each of them works—and to *contribute*—contribute information and ideas on how to do everything better.

You don't need an elaborate and expensive incentive-compensation system to generate this powerful force for creative change. Nor do you need consultants, software, training packages or managers with MBAs.

Everything any company needs to process the work it already does far more efficiently is already in the minds, hands and experience of the workers who now handle the work. They *know* where the waste is. And they are often the first to recognize new opportunities for the company to pursue.

So this book tells *how to take control* of the company and make it successful in these perilous times. And by this we do not mean control by fine-tuning financial and reporting systems, closing doors (and plants and offices) or narrowing decision-making to an expert elite.

In the simple, pencil-and-paper system described in this book, one company widened responsibility for corporate survival and profitable growth to *everyone working for the company*. The battle plan worked—and continues to work.

Everything you need to put this plan to work for yourself—in your department or in your company—is right in this book. (For free forms to make this plan easy to implement, see page 141.)

And then if we convince you to try out the ideas, go ahead. Make an earnest effort...and *then tell us what happens. We need the ideas and the problems that you and your people generate to make this system work even better.* (See page 145.)

Like all great battle plans, this one, too, can be improved by experiences...*your experiences.*

And we will take on the responsibility for adding your suggestions to this battle plan—and keeping in touch with you.

Why...

Just about 25 years ago, I started a business publication—*Boardroom Reports* (now titled *Bottom Line/ Business*)—to provide *useful and practical information* for business managers on all levels—in large, medium and smallish companies—information I had come to realize they didn't get in business schools.

They didn't get truly useful information in publications either. These focused on business gossip, Wall Street rumors and executive personalities.

During those 25 years my editors and I talked to hundreds of important and successful management consultants, business-school professors, business executives and Wall Street analysts in the US. We searched consistently for specific advice on running companies more productively, more creatively and more profitably.

Our business thrived. A $30,000 investment grew into a healthy, multimillion-dollar business. For many years I

15

was comfortably confident that we were able to provide a valuable service. And from the evidence of Boardroom's financial statements, I knew we were making money doing so.

Then, about eight years ago, I began to feel uneasy. It was becoming very evident that there were major flaws in the ways American managers were handling their businesses. And as a major advice-giver to America's managers, that meant there were flaws in the advice we were seeking out and publishing.

American companies had once seemed so invincible. We had the ability to innovate, to transfer these ideas by means of efficient mass production, to control fast-growing, increasingly complex organizations by scientific management. Most of all, we had the ability to provide our workers with higher and higher standards of living.

Suddenly we appeared to be fragile. Bedrock American businesses—the auto industry, farm equipment, machine tools—were in trouble. As layoffs increased, families became more and more anxious about job security and their ability to afford adequate health care, pay for their children's college education and guarantee themselves a satisfactory retirement income. Retail business slumped. Even such high-tech American industries as computers, semiconductors and medical equipment were hurting.

My first impulse was one I shared with many of my fellow citizens: I wanted to blame the Japanese. They protected their own industries while taking advantage of the wide-open American market. Though this reaction was emotionally satisfying at first, I quickly recognized that there was nothing in it to rebuild the strength and vitality of American businesses.

Then, as I read more about how Japanese companies operated and I talked with the growing number of experts who were familiar with them, I came across ideas that *could* be used to strengthen American businesses, ideas that were far more important than whether the trading practices of Japanese firms are fair or unfair.

First, American management "experts" and American managers had been following a false trail for decades. In fact, they had diverged sharply from the trail that leads to competitive success internationally.

Second, the *right* trail—the one the Japanese had taken toward outstanding international success and truly modern management—was yet another example of American inventiveness.

The right track had been developed in the US during the 1920s. Its techniques had been crucial in building key elements of the American war machine during the 1940s. But its advocates were narrow specialists who were overwhelmed within their companies during the enormous postwar expansion of American business with its emphasis on marketing rather than production excellence.

But these specialists, including W. Edwards Deming, had been brought to Japan right after World War II by the US Army to help Japan rebuild its production capacity. And the Japanese took the advice seriously. They spent the next decade working to implement them into the fabric of business management.

You can get your company back on the right track again—the track so many American businesses went off just as the Japanese got on. That right track—the management technique you can use to succeed not only in today's global marketplace but in nonprofit work, in your family life and for your personal goals—is the subject of this book.

Anyone can apply it—in large and small operations, from the top or at the bottom.

Greenwich, Connecticut   Martin Edelston
July, 1998

Discoveries are often made by not following instructions,
by going off the main road, by trying the untried.
—Frank Tyger

1. "I" Power
The Perpetual
Improvement Machine

So-called "scientific management"—which encourages increasing specialization of labor on the factory floor, in research and in management—has continued to dominate American business practices long after its limitations became apparent.

Why is its grip so strong? For one thing, it works—in a rigid and limited way. And it is appealing because it imposes at least the appearance of order on complex operations. Scientific management emphasizes setting standards, then demands techniques for financial and management control to enforce those standards.

But the long-term consequences can be bitter, as many American companies have now discovered. Instead of providing the means for consistent improvement, scientific management encourages one management fad after another, each promising to shock the company into higher performance. It has led to dangerous arrogance about American innovative genius and its ability to keep the

19

nation's companies competitively strong. And it tempts managers into short-term thinking and into devising short-term incentives.

For the most successful Japanese companies, there is only one system: *Kaizen*—continuous improvement. Not a day goes by without meaningful improvement in companies that use Kaizen. They have to use it in order to stay competitive and remain valued suppliers of goods and services.

Contrast: When, as is true of many US companies, the emphasis is on setting standards and establishing controls, all the energy and drive in a company is assumed to flow downward—from management—chiefly in the form of "big ideas"—more often as *this year's* big idea.

But the day-in-day-out process of Kaizen—of continuous improvement—requires successful implementation of *a series of ideas*—large, small and also those in between. And that involves every person in the company—at every level—in thinking about the process of work and suggesting and implementing improvements.

The techniques for continuous improvement started in America in the 1920s. How did such a simple, powerful idea get lost in America? Does it still make sense for American business? Can continuous improvement be implemented in US companies?

Yes! And the sooner your company adopts it, the better off it will be.

This book explains the simple way in which we successfully created such a system at Boardroom. We actually reinvented the system—and only after putting it together did we recognize that it was essentially the Kaizen system.

We call it "I" Power.

Any company—large or small—can use it. Any department, group or individual in any company can use it.

• As an individual, you can use "I" Power to make any job more productive—and more creative and interesting.

• As a first-level manager, you can use "I" Power to noticeably improve the performance of a working group.

• As a company, you can use "I" Power to sharpen your competitive edge and assure it the flexibility it needs to survive in today's business world.

Continuous improvement works for nonprofit organizations—large and small—and even for families. Individuals can use the system to improve their own business and/or personal expectations.

Back in the beginning of developing a new management system at Boardroom, we had arrived at a method, but we didn't have a name for it. We ran a company-wide contest—a way of finding a name that was, as you shall see, the essence of "I" Power itself.

As the suggestions came pouring in, many of the names began with the letter "i." Words like "ideas," "innovation," "improvement," "incentive," "ingenuity," "individual," "inspiration."

The "I" in "I" Power stands for that long list. But more important, it stands for that very simple pronoun that is the source of all that power: "I."

Two ways to make "I" Power work for you

• *Give up the illusion of scientific management that all good ideas for improving company performance flow from the top.*

• *Recognize that change for the better is more important than conforming to standards.*

The most important thing in communication is to hear what isn't being said.

—Peter F. Drucker

2. Everyone Goes In...Nothing Comes Out
The Company Meeting As A Corporate Black Hole

"How are the meetings at your company?"

It was an offhand question, put to me at the end of a long day of consultation by Peter Drucker, and I answered it frankly.

"They're pretty bad," I said, before I hastened to qualify myself. "But aren't meetings at all companies pretty bad?"

Then Drucker made a simple suggestion. Properly implemented, it transformed our company in less than two years.

It has tremendously improved the productivity and effectiveness of *all* our business meetings and, more importantly, all of our business operations.

It has changed the way people at Boardroom *think* about their work. At every level in the company, our people now think consciously or unconsciously about improving the way they work much of the time they're awake...about more efficient ways of organizing the flow

23

of work, about improving quality, about saving money without reducing the quality of our products and services, about improving service to our customers, about helping one another work to our best capacity. And that creative thinking helps in our personal lives, too.

Peter Drucker's suggestion: *Have everyone who comes to a meeting be prepared to give two ideas for making his/her own or the department's work more productive...ideas that will enhance the company as a whole.*

ONE STEP FORWARD. ONE STEP BACK

Drucker's idea made a lot of sense. It vibrated with essential truth. It had the characteristic of all good ideas: It seemed to be at once both new and obvious.

It was easy to feel that it would be good for people in our company to make some continuous connection, to have regular ways to talk constructively with one another. We had never had much of a program for doing that.

So we started out immediately after my meeting with Drucker—simply and clumsily.

I called a meeting with a group of our people from various levels of the company and put down as #1 on the agenda: *Three ideas from each person about improving work, saving money or making money.* (Drucker had suggested two ideas, but, driving for improvement, I tried for a 50% productivity increase right away.)

People at the meeting threw out ideas with great enthusiasm. One of the newest—and one of our lowest-paid—associates made one of the best suggestions ever at that meeting.

Finally, I had been to a meeting I really enjoyed.

But I wasn't prepared for such a flow of ideas. I took detailed notes, lost some right away and couldn't remember others. As a result, I wound up awed by the power of the ideas but felt guilty, chagrined and embarrassed that I couldn't make them happen. I didn't know *how* to make them happen. Ultimately, almost all of these initial ideas were lost because we didn't have a *structure and process in place to make sure these things got done.*

TWO STEPS FORWARD

After two more exciting but frustrating meetings, I put it all aside. I couldn't bring even a few of the most workable ideas to life...and I didn't have to. We were doing fabulously without them. Boardroom's business was booming.

Then something happened. In analyzing our numbers closely, one of our consultants found that we had been spoiled by success. We had gotten very fat. To secure our future, we had to cut back on staff—*now!*

I made a substantial cutback in personnel. Eventually almost half of the staff was pared away. I was, of course, very troubled by having to let people go.

I had made mistakes. Others had made mistakes. I didn't want to make those mistakes again. How could Boardroom operate more efficiently, more consistently?

During this difficult time I was haunted by the gold mine of ideas that had never been executed. I realized that I had missed a great opportunity...but there was a second chance to grab it.

So one weekend I thought through the entire plan. I wrote it out in great detail—step by step. Then I discussed it at length with our Executive Committee. We started up the idea program again—in a form that has required only minor refinements since then.

"I" Power and timing

When times are good, you'll find that it's easy to think you don't need any more ideas on how to make things better. But a consistent flow of good ideas can keep the good times from turning bad.

Ideas are like rabbits. You get a couple and learn how to handle them, and pretty soon you have a dozen.

—John Steinbeck

3. The Gong Show ...Or a Little Bit of Corporate Cabaret

I turned up at the first new series of meetings with a stack of dollar bills and handfuls of wrapped candies. I also had a big gong and a hunter's horn to salute each idea as it was presented.

For a reasonable idea, I struck the gong once and handed out a $1 bill.

For a better idea, I struck twice and handed out $2.

I honked the horn for ideas I thought were flawed—and handed out candy.

And we assigned someone to write down the ideas.

As loopy as this performance sounds, it worked—or at least most of it did.

The honking horn was dropped almost immediately because it raised negative feelings in people, even when the horn was honking for someone else. The system of positive reinforcements, however, worked well then and continues to do so to this day. It provides not only immediate behaviorist carrots but a whole reward apparatus

27

—until ideas and innovation are associated with success and favor in the minds of every single employee of the company.

Let me go back a moment to the fact that we dropped the horn honk as a signal of disapproval. This was an extremely important move, because it symbolized the removal of negative judgments from the process.

I cannot stress this enough. In order to foster a flow of ideas, the atmosphere must be totally free of negativity. People must feel comfortable about saying things right off the top of their head, since that's where some of the best ideas come from anyway.

We now award a $1 minimum for any idea—good, bad or ugly—right at the meeting. Immeasurably more important than the few dollars wasted on unworkable ideas is the receptive, wide-open, go-for-it mood that's created.

No idea is criticized at the meeting. In fact, for the most part we don't even *discuss* the merits of an idea there. Occasionally there is a brief constructive question or comment. But the emphasis is on *flow*. And that generates a continuous, glowing, positive atmosphere.

RUNNING A MEETING

When I or any other manager runs a meeting, we walk around the table with a pocket full of bills. We've learned by practice that the chief value of the small monetary awards is to create a bit of theater. To change the pace:

- Sometimes we'll give a $10 bill to someone who suggests a very good idea.
- A few times, I've torn a bill in half and given one part to the person with the idea—and promised the other half when he/she implements the idea.

Lesson: Having ideas on how to make work more productive *is fun—real fun.* It's exciting. It's invigorating. It's just that simple.

Thinking up ideas is not some grim task designed to exploit everyone's resources of energy and good, common sense. *Workers want to share their ideas on how to do their jobs better. We're all in this together.*

They have loads of ideas!

EVERY MEETING IS AN OPPORTUNITY

At an "I" Power meeting, anyone can *pass* when his/her turn comes up. At the beginning of each meeting they are reminded that they can pass—but few do now. The more good ideas that come forth, the more good ideas they create.

Meetings called specifically to generate ideas are only part of the process. In fact, these meetings may be important in only the first months of an "I" Power program—to get everyone comfortable with the experience and start them thinking about ways to do the job better as they work.

Over time, *every* business meeting becomes an opportunity to generate ideas.

The traditional weekly department meeting called to get everyone up-to-date on priorities and schedules and to track progress is an ideal forum in which to press for ideas from *everyone.* (See Chapter 11.) And so are regular meetings of senior managers.

In a remarkably short time, sterile or tense meetings will all be transformed into perpetual improvement machines.

WHAT TO DO WITH ALL THE GOOD IDEAS

Right at the start, you must be ready to commit people and time to handle the flow of ideas so that:

    • Everyone who makes a suggestion gets a quick response—within seven days at the most.

• Good ideas are rapidly implemented.

Response and implementation provide people with the *personal* satisfaction that keeps them generating new ideas. Yes, people want the operations on which they work to go more smoothly, more productively, more accurately. They are encouraged by seeing their own suggestions put in place—and working successfully.

THE TRACKING SYSTEM FOR IDEAS

1. Prepare short suggestion forms—print or photocopy them—and have them available at every meeting and at key spots in the organization. The form should have a space for the name of the person who submitted the idea.

It will save time if a code is also printed on the back of the form so that the person evaluating ideas can quickly check off what is to be done about the suggestion.

The form (size: $2\frac{3}{4}''H \times 3\frac{3}{4}''W$) and codes we use at Boardroom look like this:

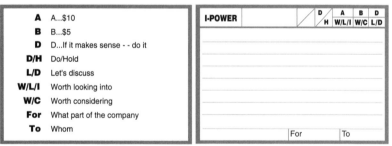

See page 141 for free copies of this form, along with other tools to start an "I" Power program in your organization.

2. Put a receptacle on the table at every company meeting into which people can drop ideas generated by the meeting.

At the end of each meeting, promptly gather up the ideas and put them in a common receptacle. Also put a few marked receptacles around the company at key spots so people can sit down, write down an idea and drop it right in.

3. Once a week, remove the idea forms from the receptacles and affix them to $8\frac{1}{2}" \times 11"$ sheets of three-holed paper. Arrange them so that all ideas submitted by an individual are together. Put the pages in a three-ring binder. Our idea forms were sized to fit three to six on a page.

4. Assign a person—as senior an executive as possible —to review all the ideas, make rewards, comment and ask for more information if necessary. This review *must* be done at least once a week—*without fail.* For the first few years I personally evaluated each idea—every weekend. Now that the flow is so great we have more people reviewing ideas.

5. Right after the review, assign someone to make up envelopes with individual cash rewards. Immediately distribute the rewards *personally* to the people who made the suggestions. Make this a regular weekly assignment for someone. *Best:* Print or stamp something on the envelope to make it special. Enclose a personal note of thanks for the useful idea.

6. Prepare a monthly report on suggestions for the entire staff (at Boardroom we just call it an *"I" Power Winners Report*). *Report:*

a. Total number of suggestions submitted that month.

b. First-place idea for the month. Name of the person and summary of the suggestion. *Reward:* Two tickets to an entertainment or sports event of their choice. Or dinner for two at a local restaurant.

c. Person with the most A-rated suggestions for the month. *Reward:* $50.

d. Summary of *every* A-rated suggestion made that month.

7. Prepare a monthly report on implementation of

ideas (at Boardroom we call it the *"I" Power Accomplishments Report*). Summarize ideas. Name the person behind each suggestion. Briefly describe the actions taken.

"I" Power thrives on...

• *Encouragement. Simply having an idea about how work might be done better is valuable. It means that people are thinking about the process. With experience and practice, the quality of ideas improves.*

• *Follow-through. A quick response and an immediate reward are essential.*

• *Top-level attention. Reviewing ideas and making sure they are responded to is a high-level manager's job.*

An educated man is one on whom nothing is lost.
—Wendell Smith

4. Why the Eagle Guards Its Nest
Keeping Track of Ideas

Ideas burst like fireworks at the beginning of almost every company suggestion program. But then they almost always sputter downward like spent rockets...until a new reward system or some other gimmick starts the pattern over again.

Contrast that with what is happening with "I" Power at Boardroom. After nine years of implementing the program, we are getting *more ideas per person* than we ever did. *Average now:* More than 100 ideas from each person over 12 months. And the numbers keep climbing.

At a recent business meeting, about 40 of our people, divided into seven opportunity groups, generated *hundreds* of ideas. The output was so startling that we didn't run it through our "I" Power system. We just gave the ideas directly to specific managers to implement.

We will generate more than 150 ideas per person over the next 12 months.

At the average US firm with a suggestion plan,

however, the rate is only one suggestion per year for every seven employees.

One hundred ideas per person is about equal to what Mitsubishi gets from its employees in a much more diversified working environment. Our rate is better than the suggestion rate at Toyota, Canon or Pioneer.

MODEST REWARDS

We generate this response despite offering very modest cash rewards for ideas:

• One to ten dollars distributed at idea meetings and monthly awards.

• Fifty dollars for those who contribute the greatest number of A-rated ideas that month.

• Two tickets to any show in town for the best idea of the month.

Key: We show respect and appreciation for the thinking that goes into *each* idea by spending management time and money to keep track of the ideas—and by implementing them *promptly*.

MAKING IT EASY

When we first initiated "I" Power meetings, one person at each meeting was assigned the task of writing down each idea as it was presented. Pretty quickly, though, we came up with a way to make employees themselves responsible for writing up their ideas—in a very simple way.

Each person now writes down each suggestion (and his/her name) on the simple "I" Power suggestion forms.

They can drop the forms into a giant top hat that sits prominently on a table in our main reception area, through which everyone passes at least half a dozen times a day.

We make sure that the forms are available at every meeting where we expect ideas to be generated so that people can write their ideas down immediately. And we also place a big fish bowl for ideas in the middle of the meeting table.

REVIEWING IDEAS

At the end of the week, an office assistant puts the "I" Power forms—three to six on a page—on $8\frac{1}{2}" \times 11"$ sheets of three-holed paper. The assistant arranges the pages alphabetically by workers' names.

For at least two years, I reviewed each idea personally. Now I share the task, but we all follow the same routine.

The sheets go into a clearly marked folder and then into a priority place in the briefcase of work that I take home every Friday evening.

Over the weekend—usually while I'm on my exercise bicycle—I go through the folder carefully. I never spend less than an hour on the task—and often more. With a colored pen, I simply circle the code letter at the top right-hand corner of the form to indicate what action to take.

On Monday the pages of suggestions, with comments, are photocopied. And the comments immediately go back to the person who made the suggestion. Right then and there, each one knows whether the idea will be acted on or not.

A ideas are certainly good enough to be implemented.

And "W/L/I" (Worth Looking Into) on B ideas is a polite "Okay—Go ahead and gather the information needed to make a decision."

The "I" Power coordinator immediately takes action on the ideas that can be implemented quickly. He/she sets up a file for each idea that will require additional work—a purchase or a discussion with members of another department, with a supplier, etc.

I've made it clear to everyone in the company—in meetings, by memo and by personal conversation—that anyone can either speak to me directly or write me a follow-up note if he/she disagrees with an evaluation of his/her ideas.

Anyone who wants to present an idea again with more information is more than welcome to do so.

Keeping track of "I" Power ideas and following up on implementation of the more complex suggestions are priority tasks for a seasoned manager and an assistant.

As chief executive and owner of the company, I'm saying to each employee: *This is important. It's worth spending money on.*

Treat ideas with respect

• *Make sure reviewing, implementing and rewarding suggestions is a priority task for an executive (or executives) with high stature in the eyes of all employees.*

• *Use specifically designed forms for suggestions so that ideas are presented succinctly and can be reviewed—and revised when necessary—efficiently.*

• *Gather suggestions immediately after every meeting and make sure they are assembled for review with care.*

I believe that all really worthwhile managerial learning takes place through personal observation, provided that there is some sort of context within which real-world encounters can be placed.

—Paul Strassmann

5. Follow Up, Follow Up, Follow Up ...Or Else

In any company like ours that runs lean and hard, good ideas can get lost because they are put aside to keep day-to-day activities moving along.

For any manager who wants to raise the odds that improvements identified by the "I" Power system will be implemented in a timely fashion, I recommend two tools that have been enormously valuable to me:

• *Tickler file.* I keep a recording device with me most of the time and dictate short memos to individuals (or to myself), with copies to be filed in my personal tickler file—with a date for follow-up action. I end every day by reviewing my list of priorities and the next day's tickler file as I set my priorities for the day's work. Sometimes all I need to do is dictate another short memo to a specific person, asking him/her to get me up-to-date promptly on progress on the project.

New computer programs function just as my manual tickler file does, presenting a flashing reminder note when a specific day comes around.

• *Follow-up sheet.* I've arranged the names of key people geographically on my follow-up sheet—that is, by the location of their offices. I fill out the follow-up sheet with notes from that day's tickler file.

We don't waste a lot of time rounding up people for time-wasting meetings to report progress. Several times a day I meet people in their offices and use my follow-up sheet to focus discussions. That gets me up-to-date much faster than any meeting—and it's much more energizing.

I also make personal visits simply to encourage action. I follow the clues on my follow-up sheet, moving easily from department to department with a clear idea of what my priorities in each one are.

Personal "I" Power lesson

If you get distracted and forget about encouraging and responding to ideas, those who work for you will stop generating them. And the fault will be yours, not theirs.

Change starts when someone sees the next step.
—William Drayton

6. The Most Important Chapter of This Book

Most executives need a simple, pared-down précis of a program or strategy, something they can grasp and act upon in an immediate, basic way.

These seven steps present the way to implement "I" Power in a series of clear, direct procedures.

I. Present "I" Power to key people. Have them read this "I" Power book. Discuss it at a lunch meeting. Follow up with a 30-minute meeting to answer questions. Each person must bring two or three questions.

II. Appoint "I" Power People

1. *"I" Power director for each department:* To set the pace, head the meetings and be responsible for coming up with themes for the meetings. Determining priorities. Evaluating important suggestions. This is only a small

part of the manager's job. The best person for the job is the head of the department.

2. *"I" Power coordinator for each department:* Supervises collection of the suggestions. Supervises the organization of the suggestions. Follows through. Evaluates the less important suggestions. Directs all approved suggestions to those who can best implement the ideas. This is not a full-time job. It is part of an efficient manager's job.

3. *"I" Power data manager:* This is part of a clerical job. Put all ideas on sheets as directed by the coordinator—for evaluation by director or coordinator. Gather all ideas by individuals. Keep track of data on ideas by individual, by month, year-to-date.

III. "I" Power meetings with up to 20 top people.

Ten to 15 people is probably tops at first, until people gain experience in running this kind of meeting.

1. Each person comes to the meeting with three suggestions. The ideas should be responsive to the focus set by the invitation to the meeting.

2. The participants write down their suggestions and drop them into the "I" Power bowl (or box, file, etc.) at the table.

3. The director kicks off the meeting by awarding "I" Power ideas with small cash prizes: $1 minimum, $2 or more for better ideas, almost never more than $10.

4. Coordinators collect suggestions after the meeting —and proceed with their work.

IV. Troubleshooting: Focusing on problem units.

1. Director meets with top two people in a problem group. (One or both were probably at the preceding "I" Power meeting.)

2. Identify the problems that the group should use "I" Power to solve (e.g., quality, late delivery, lagging sales, absenteeism, spirit, etc.).

3. Ask for a typed list of suggestions each week. How many suggestions or ideas are enough? I use an average of one and a half per person, so that a three-person group is expected to deliver five suggestions, a seven person group ten and so on.

4. Director meets with the "problem group" briefly (15 to 20 minutes) to review the suggestions and listen to how they are to be implemented.

V. Circulate a list of "I" Power ideas. List at top the winner of the big prize of the month, and show who came up with the most ideas.

VI. Each week report on the ideas that are being implemented. Post the report in appropriate places.

VII. Challenge the foot-draggers. If you're not averaging one idea per person, per week, ask for more. Make it a group challenge.

Failure is the foundation for success.

—Lao-tsze

7. Failure Happens

What happens if you don't succeed? If your "I" Power program doesn't take hold?

There are a handful of simple, clear, fail-safe mechanisms to fall back on if the initial effort to implement "I" Power is not successful at your company.

- Read this book again.
- Read the list on pages 39–41 very carefully.
- List what you're doing and compare it with what should be done.
- Revise your plan to make sure you are not missing any steps. (Shortcuts are the main reason for failure.)
- List the person responsible for each task on the list of what is to be done.
- Work out with each person how each item will be handled.
- Make a list of the mistakes that were made the

43

first time around.
- Get advice from as many people as possible on how to avoid repeating these mistakes.
- Start all over again: Set up a meeting with three suggestions expected from each person who attends.
- Identify two important groups (a department or a key executive group) that will be held responsible for coming up with at least one idea per individual each week.
- Follow up each suggestion with personal contacts and notes.

Guarantee

You will generate useful ideas.

*Give me a good fruitful error any time, full of seeds,
bursting with its own corrections. You can keep your sterile
truth for yourself.*

—Vilfredo Pareto

8. "I" Power Meltdown Or What You Can Learn From Failure

I've informally introduced the "I" Power idea to a few business friends. Some are doing well with it. Others got something out of it, but far less than we do at Boardroom. And with some, it was a failure.

These efforts have given me an understanding of the way "I" Power can fail. *But failure is never the result of workers having too few ideas.*

The problem is that most managers don't want to devote consistent effort to the detailed work and the follow-up on implementation that makes "I" Power effective.

IT WASN'T JUST THE 25 CENTS

One head of a company who succeeded heard about "I" Power and invited me to tell his 20 top executives about it recently. It was the first time I had talked about the system in public. I briefly described what we did, and they seemed fairly interested. So I asked the president if it would be all right if I went around the big table and asked each executive to come up with just one idea on how he/she could become more effective.

Once the president gave me the go-ahead, the ideas began to pour out. I wasn't prepared with a pile of dollar bills…but I had grabbed some rolls of quarters before leaving the office. Some executives collected two or three quarters for very powerful ideas.

What helped prime the pump: The president himself started with a very simple but meaningful idea about how he could use his business time more effectively.

We were all astonished, I think, to see how responsive these highly compensated executives were to so little monetary reward. Money—obviously—was not the incentive. The creativity in each person was there and was just waiting for a chance to break out.

A FALSE START

Another friend, with a business in the $100 million sales range, also tried "I" Power. Proudly, he told me he had collected more than a dozen ideas in one month and that the executives had a great time figuring out who to give the award to that month.

Well, 12 ideas is better than no ideas. But we get dozens and dozens of ideas *at a single meeting.* Several of our people average more than a dozen prize-winning ideas a month—individually.

I'm sure the ideas are there too at my friend's company.

What went wrong here? The head of the company delegated the project. He didn't make it clear that this was a priority program—and a *continuing* one. Nor did he insist that the person in charge stick to each of the system's dynamic details. So it went the way of many suggestion systems—just about nowhere.

AN APPETIZER

The failure to succeed with "I" Power that distresses me the most is that of an enormously successful Manhattan restaurant—and my favorite. Business had been falling off and the proprietor, whom I've come to know well, complained to me about it. I saw a fine opportunity to apply "I" Power and prepared a step-by-step outline for him on what he might do to improve the situation.

He held one meeting and sent me the results. The ideas from waiters, cooks, captains—everyone—were staggeringly good. I see the results of just one contribution every time I dine there nowadays. Someone suggested that they would make much more money by having San Pelligrino water available only in small bottles, not in the big ones—and that's what they do now. Members of the staff who knew my role in suggesting the meeting told me how successful they thought it had been.

But my friend, the proprietor, believes that running a fine restaurant is an art, not a business. He hasn't been able to bring himself to keep up the meetings—and keep up the suggestions.

"I" Power Failure???

The system doesn't fail...The failures fail to follow the simple steps.

In the race for quality, there is no finish line.

—David Kearns

9. America, Phone Home

Tapping into the skills and knowledge of workers who, day in and day out, handle the actual work in offices and factories is the most powerful—and underutilized— engine of growth, ideas, strength and opportunity available to every American company.

What the simple, easy-to-use "I" Power system does is return to common-sense practices innovated by many American companies in the lusty era when they were rapidly overtaking all the older industrial powers in the world.

If the essence of "I" Power is indeed that simple—idea and follow-up—by now you are probably asking the obvious question: What happened? How could such an exquisite method of ensuring the long-term health of a company not be recognized, cherished, implemented and refined?

Eastman Kodak established its first employee suggestion program in 1898, and it's still going strong—

invigorated in recent years by more informal, improvised suggestion systems springing up around the company. By the early 1900s, major companies—including General Electric, Westinghouse, Metropolitan Life Insurance and Parke-Davis—were encouraging employee ideas.

In more recent decades, however, suggestion systems in the few companies that had any became overly bureaucratized, slow to react and irrelevant to the massive changes companies were undergoing as a result of new, global competition and new technology.

LOOKING BACK... LOOKING AHEAD

In the 1920s and 1930s, the potential value of employee input took a major leap forward in a few American firms.

A Bell Laboratories statistician, Walter A. Shewhart, drew up some simple paper-and-pencil quality-control techniques that workers on manufacturing lines at Western Electric, where telephone equipment was made, easily learned to use. They used the new tools to recognize when adjustments to machinery or materials were necessary to maintain quality tolerances on products they were making.

This was statistical quality control (SQC), which became the basis for continuous improvement systems.

Before SQC, workers relied only on their craft and experience as guides in making adjustments in their machinery or simplifying work processes. That craft and experience were valuable. But often the workers' judgment and suggestions were overruled by supervisors.

SQC techniques gave people on the line, those who were actually doing the work, ways to measure, keep track of and make steady improvements in the quality of their output and their own productivity.

Engineering-oriented companies, such as General Electric, Westinghouse and even US auto companies, took up SQC. It became one of the essential techniques to assure quality as American industry geared up for World War II.

But a clear understanding of the power of these quality-management techniques never penetrated widely into general management in US companies. Then, after World War II, swarms of business-school-educated "professional" managers took over the middle ranks of American corporations. They put less and less value on ideas that originated on the shop floor or in clerical work pools.

THE BIG BARRIER

The growing drive was to specialize labor so that industrial engineers, armed with time-and-motion studies, could set standards for output and cost accounting. The more specialized their work became, the less workers understood how their particular job fit into the overall flow of work. And postwar top managements of US companies, with the world hungry for their goods, focused on marketing, on financial controls, on decentralization or centralization of their organizations. SQC remained a toy of specialized engineers. Or it became a weapon in the hands of floor supervisors to single out workers for performing below par. Unions began to attack it. And few managers cared whether or not employees continued to use it.

Meanwhile, in postwar Japan, American occupation authorities were trying to procure vehicles and materials from local manufacturers as US defense commitments around the world increased. But well into the 1950s, the quality of Japanese production was hopelessly low.

Some army procurement officers, however, had been trained in statistical quality control in the US by W. Edwards Deming, who had long studied and admired

Shewhart's work. General Douglas MacArthur brought Deming over to teach Japanese engineers what he knew.

Japanese engineers were enthusiastic. But Deming didn't stop with them. Disappointed by the failure of American companies to adopt these techniques wholeheartedly, Deming realized that he had to convince upper management in Japanese companies of their value—or the ideas would eventually die in Japan, too.

Top managers in Japan took time to meet with Deming, and he won them over.

The Japanese miracle was set in motion. Growing consistently—one small step at a time—is how Japan became an awesome industrial power in a few decades.

One way to get everyone behind "I" Power

It's as American as apple pie.

When we would have the street cleansed, let every man sweep his own door, and it is quickly done.

—Thomas Adams

10. An Open Door Isn't Enough Anymore

Boardroom is a relatively small company. And from the start, our managers have been open-door, hands-on, walk-around practitioners...long before this behavior was recommended by management consultants.

So why did we need the "I" Power system?

Unless people are strongly encouraged to do so, they don't just pop in on their supervisors with ideas.

Nor do they bring them up at meetings. And they don't use suggestion boxes either.

They didn't even bring ideas and solutions to problems directly to me at special lunches I scheduled regularly to tune in with team members at every level of the company.

Nor did they bring them up as I wandered around sticking my nose into every activity.

I never consciously built any barriers—nor, I believe, did any of our managers. We're certainly not a bureaucratic company with layers of middle managers. In fact, *at most* there is one manager between any employee and me.

Nevertheless, once I began asking for three ideas at each meeting, they suddenly came pouring out. And everyone has been generating useful ideas at an ever-increasing pace—for more than six years.

SO, WHAT HAPPENS WITH "I" POWER?

First: Everyone recognizes that suggestions for change will not be treated as a criticism of the way things now run. Ideas are welcomed and rewarded.

And they hear that right from me, as head of the company.

No idea is ever laughed at or put down in any way.

Second: Response to suggestions is reliably timely.

As one of our people told me: "When I figure that a new computer printer would be helpful for a department, I could write you a memo, prepare a proposal...or simply describe in a couple of sentences through "I" Power what it would do. I do it through "I" Power because I know for certain that you read each suggestion—fast. And I'll have my answer the next week."

Third: Individuals don't have to calculate the best time or the best way to personally present their ideas to a manager.

No matter how informally and fairly managers deal with those who report to them, or with their peers, it's hard for most people to step beyond the boundaries they perceive, or expect to confront, beyond their own job turf, their own areas of responsibility and authority.

What "I" Power makes clear is that making things work better anywhere in the company is in everyone's self-interest.

People dare to think. I've found that fresh and original ideas for publications, books, headlines and titles originate with about as much frequency and quality from typesetters and office-service workers as from editors or experienced marketers. And a clerk who asks a simple, common-sense question can uncover astonishing ways to save hundreds of thousands of dollars on postage—annually.

THERE ARE NO BOUNDARIES TO COMMON SENSE

Of course, this requires top managers who are open to new ideas, no matter where they come from, and who are ready to shed the rigid hierarchies of corporate culture to adopt a more fluid, practical approach to their jobs. "Scientific management" is relatively simple: Memorize and enforce a handful of hard-and-fast rules. "I" Power management is in a sense "messier." No organization chart prevents a file clerk from originating an idea that can be implemented company-wide.

When an idea for continuous improvement in one part of our company comes from someone in an entirely different part of the company, that's great! People can't protect their old ways of doing business anymore. Good ideas move with their own power, not on the impetus of any originator's name that is attached to them.

It is a challenging, heady "new corporate order" that "I" Power has brought to Boardroom.

Everyone is now everyone else's boss.

Employees make suggestions on how I can improve my own effectiveness, too.

Sometimes an "I" Power idea is so personal that the originator considers it clumsy or undiplomatic to make the suggestion publicly. We've built a way to make anonymous suggestions through "I" Power even though we don't get many. Every anonymous suggestion thus far has proved to be worthy of careful attention. Awards for anonymous "I" Power ideas go into a fund for a local charity. Of course, those who see their anonymous ideas implemented get plenty of personal satisfaction.

Every company that embraces the idea of continuous improvement soon recognizes what a barrier functional turf and hierarchical titles are to top performance.

Eventually I would like to adopt the system developed by an entrepreneur-acquaintance of mine. At his very successful company, nobody has a job title. Of course, people know what departments they work in and what their duties are. They simply don't have titles. He developed his company that way right from the start.

I started my own company using the more conventional system of titles and functions. Now I find it difficult to move, as I would like to move, to the more open structure.

We may do it eventually, though, despite the pressures for hierarchical and functional distinctions that are still forced on us by the society in which we live.

If the "I" Power new corporate order threatens your preconceived sense of order

All I can say is, snap out of it! The real threat is from our new competitors, and they aren't stopping to cherish tired old notions of propriety and hierarchical niceties.

Almost all really new ideas have a certain aspect of foolishness when they are first produced, and almost any idea which jogs you out of your current abstractions may be better than nothing.

—A.N. Whitehead

11. Thinking
The Subject That No School in America Teaches

I would like "three ideas from everyone" to be #1 on the agenda of virtually every meeting at Boardroom—whether I run the meeting or not. But that's not the case.

Some managers just don't seem to be comfortable running a meeting with a handful of dollar bills, rewarding the source of each idea as it emerges. That's okay.

Our managers know how valuable suggestions for improvement are...and they get those suggestions any way that they are comfortable about getting them.

One manager, for instance, objected to the "pressure" of having to come up with three ideas at a meeting. It should be voluntary, she said. If you press people too hard, she felt, they will deliver trivial ideas just to meet the quota.

But what does she do at the weekly meetings she has with the people who report to her?

Her words: I don't insist that they bring in any ideas.

We always set aside five minutes at the end of each meeting, though, to brainstorm ideas on how to make our operation better.

We want to stay in the habit of thinking of ways to get things done better…We want to follow up to make sure the better ways are implemented.

That's our job. *Then,* after the meeting, many of the people drop the ideas they came up with in the "I" Power top hat. That strengthens support for the idea…gives recognition. And the little envelope with cash once a month tangibly tells each of us, in a different way, that it pays to think.

What will make "I" Power work for you

Flexibility. If you expect your top managers to be flexible and have a fluid approach to corporate structure, you have to measure up to the same criterion. This manager's approach to eliciting "I" Power suggestions is somewhat different from mine. But the result is the same, so why should I care?

Time has a wonderful way of weeding out the trivial.
—Richard Ben Sapir

12. Nontrivial Pursuit Or Why No Idea Is Too Small for "I" Power

Let's go back to that manager's complaint about "trivial" ideas. Isn't it true that some suggestions are just too insignificant to waste time over?

From time to time we survey our team for suggestions on how to improve upon the "I" Power program at Boardroom, and this is invariably the leading criticism that comes up.

Some ideas are so trivial, the complaint says, that they don't deserve any monetary award, not even a small one. I even remember a specific example to which objections were raised: One employee had received the customary $1 award for saying, "I need a bigger wastebasket."

I have found, however, that no idea is too small for me to pay attention to.

Every idea to improve the way work or conditions of work in the company are handled has several dimensions:

1. *The idea itself*—which may or may not be very useful or practical or have bigger implications.

2. The encouragement to everyone—to continually think about change and about making things better at work.

3. The acknowledgment that top management cares about the people who work in the organization. Taking care of the little things proves that even better than implementing the big winners.

4. The development of a work force that thinks about change—and is responsive to change recommended by others. Resistance is the standard in most workplaces. Responsiveness alone puts an organization ahead competitively.

WRONG ASSUMPTIONS

Nothing costs the company more in the long run than a staff of people who simply take orders and do exactly what they're told to do. Or who fear and resist any change in what they do or the way they do it.

The standard errors by top managers in America:

• *Arrogance.* Thinking that all ideas for improvement come from professional managers.

• *Complacence.* Thinking that employees will naturally suggest any ideas they come up with to improve the way they do their work.

In the nation's oldest corporate suggestion system— and one of the most generous—at Kodak, employees were rewarded only for ideas *outside* their own area of work because they were "expected" to suggest those closer to home.

These assumptions about the natural behavior of managers and employees are contradictory. And they're *both* wrong.

Everyone profits from being intelligently encouraged to observe what they do. And everyone profits from thinking about ways to improve the way they've been trained to work. Training that doesn't encourage this is actually harmful.

If someone figures out that additional staplers or wastebaskets around the workplace will keep the work flowing faster, that's not a trivial idea.

It's not simply a joke to suggest giving a humorous name to each copy machine on the floor so it will be easier for us to identify the machine that needs service or supplies.

No idea is too small to deserve the encouragement it gives people to keep thinking.

When people complain to me that some employees are making a contest out of "I" Power ideas—trying to maximize the number of suggestions they make (even though almost all are small) in order to maximize the dollars they collect—I let them know that I'm very happy with that. The more ideas, the better. May the little ones lay the groundwork for big ones. May employees always show the way for management.

The more "I" Power ideas the better

Ideas provide the input. Ideas contribute to an attitude of change.

A man who was leading the way through a river was asked if the water was deep. He replied: The result itself will show.

—Plato

13. Is It Your Job Or Is It "I" Power?

Once "I" Power breaks the ice and ideas begin to flow, managers play a key role in guiding members of their teams to distinguish between doing their jobs well and identifying ways to *improve* the job process.

Here's how one of Boardroom's most thoughtful managers explains what he does:

We recently changed vendors—to a major supplier whose invoices would be much more complex than the ones we were used to. At our weekly meeting, one of the people in my unit offered as an "I" Power idea: Let's go over the first invoices from the new vendor line by line to make sure they're accurate.

While checking the bills might have seemed to be just part of this person's job, this preplanning made the process more effective.

The following week the same person proposed: The new vendor's forms aren't clearly designed. Let's reformat them so they're more user-friendly. Then we would be less likely to make mistakes when checking them out.

That was an even higher level of improvement, I thought. Okay, submit it as an "I" Power idea. (It was accepted, implemented and produced a modest gain.)

By now the distinction between doing the expected thoroughly and figuring out a better way to avoid errors was becoming clearer to the person.

Not surprisingly, the following week the same worker came through with an "I" Power idea that showed forward thinking and an understanding of what *significant* improvement is. It avoided substantial potential waste and produces continuing savings for us.

She suggested that we prepare in advance to bar-code envelopes so we would be ready to qualify for sizable upcoming postal discounts. Since we already knew what the new post-office–approved specifications were, we could design envelopes well ahead of time. Then we wouldn't wind up with wasted inventory of envelopes that did not qualify for the discount. And we would be sure not to miss the discount on any mailings.

Bingo! A big one!

We implemented the suggestion—and the post office used some of our envelopes as models for the industry.

Three "I" Power ideas from the same person. One involved doing her expected job better. One involved a slight innovation. The third produced significant gains for the company.

What's important, in "I" Power terms, is not so much the end result of the ideas but the fact that this worker was encouraged to think about ways to innovate on the job. She had become an engaged, contributing employee.

If our manager had stopped to pass value judgments on each of her ideas—this one is not so good, this one is better but just part of your job, this one is trivial—she might have lost her zest in offering suggestions. She would have become her own censor, second-guessing each idea she had. "Well, they didn't think the reformatting idea was so hot," she'd say to herself, "maybe I'd better clam up about the envelopes for the new postal regulations."

You don't want that. To use "I" Power effectively, you must foster the flow of ideas among your employees. And to do that, you must value every suggestion without immediately linking its value to its eventual result.

Foster the continuous flow of "I" Power ideas

Value every suggestion. The process is more important than the particulars.

In the morning sow thy seed, and till evening let not thy hand rest, for thou knowest not which will succeed, this or that, or whether both alike shall be good.

—Ecclesiastes
As translated by Morris Jastrow

14. What's the Motive Behind a Good Suggestion? Should You Care?

People make "I" Power suggestions just to get noticed, I'm sometimes told. And that's great.

Some of them just want to make sure I know they're doing things. And that's great.

For many of them it's really only the $10 here...the $5 there. And that's great, too.

Some team members put ideas into the "I" Power top hat that are such obvious and quick improvements in the way they do their work that they've already started to implement the change. Making changes like that has just become part of doing their jobs better. But they figure it might be wiser to let me know about it. (I gather I've never disagreed with any of these suggestions in my weekly ratings of "I" Power ideas.)

What's wrong with any of these motives?

Nothing! It's all great. It keeps us getting better and better...every day...in many ways.

> ## What to do when an "I" Power idea from one person affects other people's work or the work of another department

Don't waste time and energy on figuring out the "politics." Encourage everyone involved to discuss the idea and recommend a solution or course of action.

Them as will, can.

—Old saying

15. We Want More!
And...More!
...And More!

What about paying for ideas that employees "should" be submitting entirely voluntarily?

Our experience is that people have to be encouraged—even pushed—hard! Many people hold back their ideas for many of the same reasons they hold back from entering the manager's open door.

So this is the letter that we send out a few times a year to those people who seem to be sending in a below-average number of ideas.

Dear _____,

We have studied the number of "I" Power suggestions submitted by members of the Boardroom team from *[date]* to *[date]*.

The average total of suggestions per person is now slightly over _____. That includes high-suggestion-count contributors, low-suggestion-count contributors and your ____ contributions.

More ideas from you would help us all—and you, too. So...ideas, please, on:

• How can you operate more effectively?

• How can your whole department operate more effectively?

The future for all of us is up to each of us…and we're looking forward to more help from you.

Can you push too hard for more "I" Power ideas?

No. But you can encourage the flow of ideas toward company priorities.

Crisis is another name for opportunity.

—Anonymous

16. "I" Power Pays Off
A Boardroom Case Study
...The Problem

"I" Power had been in place at Boardroom for less than one year when we were unexpectedly faced with making urgent changes in several key areas of operation.

The dollar payoff from "I" Power suggestions had long been apparent. Now, in a dramatic way, we experienced for the first time how "I" Power had upgraded the capacity of Boardroom team members to recognize a problem and solve it—in record time.

In less than three months we:

• Changed our biggest single supplier—the printer of our publications.

• Radically changed the process and technology we use to produce our biggest circulation publications.

• Saved hundreds of thousands of dollars a year because the techniques we worked out with the new printer enabled us to take advantage of postal discounts.

Everyone at Boardroom involved in recognizing a problem—and the new opportunities in the change—

71

was aided by the emphasis on thinking through the process of work brought about by "I" Power.

SPOTTING A PROBLEM

One of our ongoing jobs at Boardroom is to monitor the quality of service we provide subscribers to our periodicals and buyers of our books. How soon after an order is received do we ship issues or books? How close to print date do our publications arrive in subscribers' hands?

To test this, our fulfillment manager placed orders under the names of friends and family members to monitor delivery performance.

Just before the Christmas season in 1990, she noted that the first issue of a newly ordered subscription arrived *four weeks after the date* it was to have been mailed by the printer.

Day One: Still as a regular part of her job, the fulfillment manager and an associate gathered mailing data from the printer and post office for the past few months.

Day Two: A quick review of the data revealed distressing information. The entire print run of an issue was not being mailed on the scheduled mailing date, as we assumed it was. Instead, it was being dropped off in batches at the post office *over a three-week period.* Considering that this is a *biweekly* publication, we suddenly realized that we had a serious performance problem with the vendor.

Discovery: Our publication had been a tremendous success and rapidly grew and outstripped the *mailing* capacity of the printer—though it could *print* the issues fast enough. Rather than lose us as a customer, it was doing the shipping as best it could—in batches.

FINDING A SOLUTION

As soon as the slow-delivery problem was identified, the fulfillment manager and the production manager were in my office with the facts:

    • We had to locate another printer quickly—for we had run so far beyond the capacity of our old printer that there was no way it could meet our current specifications for timely delivery. Our volume was *continuing* to grow substantially. And mailing was becoming more complex, too.

    • Our production manager had already identified several prospective suppliers but continued to look further...having found that the location from which we mailed would affect our mailing costs substantially.

Our team continued to work intensively—night and day—on postal analyses to determine the geographical location that would serve us most economically.

Less than three weeks after identifying the need for change, we selected a new printer.

This "solution," however, gave rise to a new problem: To work with the new printer, we had to completely reorganize and reequip the system we used to produce our publications. And we had to do all this in 60 days.

> ### "I" Power accelerates response time

People who are accustomed to making things work better never accept good enough as being good enough.

Collectively, human use of the concept of lessons learned has been decisive in human dominance over all other animal species.

—J.M. Juran

17. Boardroom Case Study ...The Solution

We call all the work that goes on from the time that articles and artwork are selected for each of our publications to the time the completed pages are ready to be sent to the printer *production.*

That includes cleaning up typographical errors; laying out pages; fitting copy, headlines and art to the page design; paginating; and marking pages for color, shade density and graphic effects.

It's a lot to do, under tight deadline pressure, and conflicts between productivity and quality are constant during this process.

It's my job to press continually to shorten the production cycle—lessen the human energy and the production time.

Editors and artists, however, often can't resist yet another "pass" to touch up a line or a word.

The urge is so innate, and so strong, that at one of America's preeminent publishing houses the top editor would immediately begin to pencil-edit the *printed* advance copy of the magazine when it was delivered to his desk.

As our revenues and circulation expanded and we prospered, the time we devoted to editorial production grew longer and longer—all with the aim of improving quality.

We had small early successes in reversing this trend once we began to use "I" Power. But they prepared the way for a dramatic improvement in the three-month period between Christmas 1990 and March 30, 1991, as we prepared to change to the new printer.

NO SAFETY NET

The former printer was only two hours away from our Manhattan editorial offices—westward across the Hudson River right onto a major interstate. For years that proximity had lulled us. A last-minute courier could get us out of the hole created by a production delay. Or save us from a gross mistake discovered after the issue had closed and the pages had been sent to the printer.

Our new printer was in Kentucky. We would be dependent on overnight delivery service if we continued to use our old system of production. The change could add *four days* to our production cycle if we continued to make the same number of last-minute changes. New business conditions brought new demands on our company. We had to run on a new set of rules.

- Do it right the first time.
- Send copy and graphics electronically by computer modem rather than physically on "boards."
- Convert from IBM-compatible computers to MacIntosh and train our people to use totally new software to match up with our giant new printer's systems.

•Make the whole switch fast.

FAST AND SMOOTH

Fortunately, by the time this need arose, "I" Power had given our employees two years of experience and familiarity with change and with making suggestions to improve processes.

Originally we had scheduled a switch to the new system over a six-month period.

We actually did it all in *two* months. As it turned out, we could have done it in *one* month if we had to.

We never missed a deadline. There wasn't one glitch in the first publications that went to subscribers using the new system and the new printer.

"I" Power enabled us to do it.

The editors, typesetters and artists got together... made lists of what each had to do...met briefly daily to check progress in each area. They identified problems or needs that arose quickly because they were used to communicating across functional lines. They made it work—on time.

The secret: They planned their work—and they worked their plans. They anticipated problems. They came up with creative solutions.

> **What can "I" Power deliver besides a series of small, incremental improvements?**

The power to make major changes fast—and get them right!

We all of us live too much in a circle.

—Benjamin Disraeli

18. Widening the Circle "I" Power Growth

One of the prime strategies for energizing Boardroom's "I" Power program is what I call "widening the circle." It works on the principle that the more people there are who know about "I" Power, the more successful the system will be—for you. If yours is an "I" Power company and it does business with another company that is familiar and comfortable with the precepts of "I" Power, the chances of a fruitful exchange are greatly enhanced.

We've explained and demonstrated our "I" Power program to all of Boardroom's major vendors. Most of them now regularly make suggestions to us on their own, in some cases simplifying the supply process and even cutting costs.

We simply include all of their suggestions in our monthly "I" Power reports alongside suggestions from Boardroom team members.

We push vendor participants for more ideas just as we

push people at Boardroom. And we push nonparticipating vendors to join in. We want to know from them what we can do better, based on their widespread experience.

Many of the best ideas come from vendors. They view things from a much wider perspective, bringing us the best ideas from all their customers.

The "I" Power influence goes even deeper, however.

Recently, a key member of the team that services our account at a major vendor told her "partner" at Boardroom that she was pregnant and had given notice to her company that she would not be returning from leave.

The superb performance of this vendor is essential in assuring timely delivery of our publications to subscribers. The vendor assured us that the replacement would be carefully selected and properly trained—in time, too.

The vendor selected a well-qualified person—one who was next in line for promotion for that job. It was a no-think decision. And it might have worked out. But it quickly turned out to be a problem, too. This woman was *also* pregnant and planned to take a long leave.

The vendor had no other experienced people who were ready to move in. Big problems lay ahead for us if they hired an inexperienced person—as they planned to do.

All the explanations the supplier offered were reasonable—but unacceptable to us. They came down to: "You are a very good account, but it wouldn't be fair to pull someone off another account and assign him/her to servicing yours." The supplier's managers acted as if the problem was all an act of God and they had fulfilled their responsibilities.

The traditional business solution would have been to find another vendor, but that would have caused massive transition problems.

I decided to apply "I" Power to the problem. I wrote

directly to the head of the supplier company and urged him to involve his employees in finding a solution. In that letter, and in all my subsequent contacts made toward solving this problem, I emphasized a basic principle of "I" Power.

Who knows best the requirements of this job? Conventional business practice suggests that "the personnel manager" or "the job description" explains all that. "I" Power told me differently. The supplier's own employees understood the job requirements best. They knew the work that had to be done to handle our account efficiently, what training and personal qualifications were necessary. They were the "experts," and I wanted them involved in the process from start to finish.

After intensive prodding, managers at the supplier company accepted the suggestion. They and the workers handling our account huddled, proposed, suggested, considered.

They finally came up with an ideal prospect—from a completely different part of their company. She was thoroughly experienced in the work necessary to keep our subscribers satisfied with delivery performance. She had been promoted to another part of the company, but in her current assignment work was slow. The vendor concluded that she could be spared for the necessary few months of the other employee's maternity leave. The arrangement worked out fine.

Did I make a squeaky wheel of myself so things would run smoothly? You bet I did. I insisted upon a creative solution to a potential problem—and I know just where to find that creativity: Among the workers most familiar with the tasks to be done. While creativity and "I" Power may involve effort, they have one good thing going for them: They work. The vendor has since begun a training program so that similar problems will not come up again—on our account or others.

| To leverage your own success with "I" Power |

Encourage vendors and close associates to apply the system in their own operations.

So much of what we call "management" consists in making it difficult for people to work.

—Peter Drucker

19. "I" Power Identifies The Nonproblem Problem

For many years I grappled unsuccessfully—like many other managers—with the problem of employees coming to work late. I had ruefully concluded that it was one of those situations that would be a constant battle.

For a time, I fought my side tenaciously. We installed ever more complex systems for tracking and improving arrival and departure times. We tried punishments. We tried rewards. We tried positive publicity—and negative publicity.

Once, in great frustration, I even cut back the company's voluntary contribution to profit sharing and attributed the decision directly to the lack of improvement in "the lateness problem."

When the "I" Power program encouraged employees to come up with their own ideas and solutions to problems, they also solved "our" lateness problem.

Their comments made it clear that many of the people who came in late also stayed later in the evening, worked through lunch, came in early the next day or caught up over the weekend. Our "lateness problem" was not evidence of lax performance or lack of commitment by Boardroom's employees. Most of it was due to the unpredictability of commuting to work in the congested metropolitan area. Delays were inevitable.

Lateness, for the most part, was a problem defined by management that really wasn't a problem at all.

So now we have no lateness problem.

People who come to work in the morning a few minutes late regularly or occasionally just make up the time within that week.

We've also found it possible to be quite flexible with individual schedules, permitting a few employees to come in at 10 AM and leave at 6 PM, for instance.

We have a *basic* rule for full-timers, one that allows for some measure of flexibility. Their schedules must assure that they are on hand during hours of the day when their work or presence at meetings is essential. That's it.

Don't limit "I" Power to solving problems

It can be just as useful in helping you distinguish problems from nonproblems.

Success has ruined many a man.

—Benjamin Franklin

20. Beware of Success

When our company was small there was no need to set productivity improvement goals. The initial group was amazingly productive. Teamwork came naturally because there were so few of us.

We easily crossed one another's job boundaries. Rank meant very little and didn't handicap communication because everyone at every level did plenty of scut work—including myself.

We butted into one another's areas of "expertise" with fresh questions and ideas.

We encouraged one another.

Everyone who has experienced this knows the exhilaration of being part of an effective team. The whole really is greater than the sum of its parts, as the organization becomes an organism, creating its own energy. Everyone who has experienced this knows, too, intuitively if not consciously, that this is the model of how a group should work together.

But how to transfer this synergistic, supple, organic organization to a larger frame? With growth at Boardroom came turf lines. Team members began to compete, not for higher performance but for attention, recognition, status.

When the Productivity Destroyer arrived on the scene, the ground had been well prepared.

I started up a new high-tech publication, hiring at first a very bright, two-person staff, young people recently out of college who worked under my direction. The times were right for the publication. Wall Streeters loved the newsletter. The idea took hold, and response to the publication was enthusiastic.

But because of the nature of the information we undertook to publish, each bit of copy had to be a gem— and that copy required a great deal of research and polishing. Developing each item was a Sherlock Holmes–like adventure. Find the budding breakthrough technology. Find the company furthest ahead in developing it. Identify the potential uses of the technology.

It was the stuff of Wall Streeters' dreams, but it made for a lot of work. With every writer, editor and researcher spending days to uncover and verify hard-to-get-information, the two-person staff quickly expanded to five. Then they needed their own secretary.

Other newsletter units in the growing company took notice, of course. Why shouldn't *their* staffs be as large? They produced even more pages at the same frequency. Why shouldn't *their* unit have its own secretary? If members of the high-tech team could spend so much time in the office talking to one another, why not us?

Times were good. Money was plentiful. The company was growing. I became expansive. And indulgent. Why not?

In not much more than 18 months or so, the company's total editorial staff nearly doubled. But we certainly hadn't doubled the number of publications we produced. Or the revenues. Cash flow was still good—but cash flow *projections* began to point toward trouble.

I realized that what had happened to us in a microcosm is quite similar to what had happened to virtually all American companies. The high productivity that comes almost naturally early in a company's development can't be taken for granted.

Fortunately, we didn't get into trouble before we scaled down, and we were able to create a foundation for the much healthier growth that followed.

We swiftly identified excess staffing. That took a great deal of tough thinking with my core staff once the problem became clear.

I made generous severance arrangements for the employees who were terminated as a result of my own mistakes.

Above all, I recognized the need for a continuing unifying productivity program. This was the germ of the idea that eventually became our "I" Power system.

That was ten years ago.

No new Productivity Destroyer has since been able to gain a foothold at Boardroom.

How "I" Power promotes healthy growth

"I" Power adds the fact-based, common-sense ideas and questions of people who are actually doing the work to the projections and dreams of managers.

Ask the unreasonable to get the reasonable.

—Erasmus

21. Good Hiring Made Easy

An "I" Power suggestion contributed to a major improvement in the way we now hire people at Boardroom.

In the past, we hired in the conventional way. One person, or several persons, interviewed a candidate and offered some general comment: "He's okay…She's terrific…I don't think she has what we need," etc. And we were all trapped by our own inadequacies as truly probing interviewers.

The simple suggestion: Let's list the things we're looking for in experience, skills and personality for the specific job. Then rank the candidate on each attribute… Strong…Okay…Not okay.

We now have a new drill for making hiring decisions. From the employees and managers who are most intimately acquainted with the job in question, we organize a task force that is responsible for hiring the best possible candidate. They follow a general method for every job opening.

- The team lists ten things to look for in job experience and skills, as well as five personality factors.
- Each of the people involved in making the ultimate hiring decision does a ranking.
- The team evaluates the combined ratings, discusses them and decides whether it has found someone who fits the bill or will have to look further.

Throughout the process, we continually ask ourselves crucial questions: Is there really a job here? Could parts of this job possibly be assigned to others?

Ability to learn from experience is a characteristic we need in every job, at every level, at Boardroom. Recent research suggests that it's an ability that is common to most successful executives.

Locating individuals who possess this quality is important to all companies, but probing for that quality in a recruiting interview isn't easy. What are the best questions to ask? How can an interviewer rate the candidates' learning abilities?

We've found an interviewing guide prepared by one of the nation's leading recruiters, Millington McCoy,* useful in identifying those characteristics. She has developed the following range of questions that probe a candidate's ability to learn new patterns of behavior from experience. They are based on the program of the Center for Creative Leadership.

- Tell me about a time when you tried to help someone else change. What strategy did you use? How did it turn out?
- Tell me about your most challenging and least challenging jobs.

*Millington F. McCoy is one of three managing directors of Gould, McCoy & Chadick, Inc., executive search consultants, 300 Park Ave., New York 10022.

- Tell me about a time when you had to overcome major obstacles to meet a challenge.
- Tell me about the people you most and least admire.
- Tell me about a time when you tried to do something but failed.
- Tell me about a time when something bad happened to you.
- Tell me about a mistake you made in dealing with people.
- Tell me about the best and worst course you've ever taken.
- Tell me about the last time you made a major change. Why did you do it? How did it work out?

After getting the answer to each question, rate the candidates along a scale of one to five on how they measure up to the following yardsticks.

- **Generalization.** *Weaker* candidates are more likely to generalize. It's hard to tell exactly what they learned or why they learned it. *Stronger* candidates learn something specific. They often have a good deal to say about what they learned and why.
- **Texture of learning.** *Weaker* candidates tend toward extremes. They may give bland or socially acceptable descriptions of a least-admired person, for example. At the other extreme, they may overdo blaming that person or circumstance. They don't show much texture in telling what they learned from mistakes. *Stronger* candidates are candid. They talk about mistakes and weaknesses openly. They may be quite judgmental toward themselves, situations or even other people. But they quickly move on to discuss what they did differently, or how they responded.
- **Complexity.** *Weaker* candidates have a simple

view of people and jobs. They describe fewer
nuances. *Stronger* candidates, on the other hand,
describe experience with deeper analysis. They
see more in everything than weaker candidates do.

- **Why things happened.** *Weaker* candidates focus
  more on *what* happened and much less on *why* it
  happened. They often fail to indicate that they've
  learned anything at all from the experience.
  Stronger candidates focus less on what happened
  and more on why it happened, what they learned
  and what they would do differently.
- **Recognize ambiguities.** *Weaker* candidates often
  talk about doing things right. They describe others
  in terms of what they did to them or what they got
  them to do. They use words that indicate that they
  like to control tasks and other people. *Stronger*
  candidates do not emphasize controlling others or
  perfectionism. They recognize the ambiguities of
  life.
- **Curiosity.** *Weaker* candidates ask questions about
  the context of work (chance of promotion, fringe
  benefits, etc.). *Stronger* candidates ask many
  questions about the *content* of the job.
- **Analytical honesty.** Both *strong* and *weak* candidates can analyze a failure, but *strong* candidates
  are more willing to admit their role in it. *Strong*
  candidates often admit when success was due to
  pure luck.
- **Self-awareness.** *Weaker* candidates are not particularly self-aware. They tend to overstate their
  strengths, invest too much energy in correcting
  weaknesses and are often unaware of their limits.
  Stronger candidates are aware of their strengths,
  weaknesses and limits. They're more interested in
  developing and deploying strengths and com-
  pensating for weaknesses.

"I" Power improves the quality of the hiring process

• *You involve the people who know most about the work to be done in defining the qualifications and personality needed to do the job.*

• *You continually evaluate whether you need a new or an additional person to do the work or whether the process of work can be changed and handled by a current employee.*

• *You use a consistent set of questions and rankings to establish whether a candidate meets the needs of the position.*

"You can't fire me up, so I quit."

—Andy "Taxi" Kaufman

22. When the Unreasonable Is Reasonable
Firing Through "I" Power

Using "I" Power as the engine of change, you can reduce your turnover tremendously. Occasionally, however, even after the best of efforts to match a person's strengths to the needs of the organization, you have to ask someone to leave.

How can the unsavory task of separating employee from employer be accomplished? How can the "shock to the system" that dismissal represents for both worker and company be lessened or eliminated?

The "I" Power idea: Give such a person *unreasonably* generous severance.

Giving such a person unreasonably generous severance—unreasonable, that is, from the company's point of view—turns out to be the best way to make hard decisions about termination. Oddly enough, generous severance packages actually work to keep the company financially healthy in the long run.

Every top manager has suffered the pain of delaying—

and delaying and delaying—a decision to fire a key or long-term employee when problems develop and persist with that person's performance. That delay represents a major disruption in the performance of many people.

Finally, when the situation becomes untenable, management acts. The actual firing often becomes a gross bloodletting that goes down in a crisis atmosphere. In their panic, managers make bad decisions. Everyone loses.

With a company policy of "unreasonably" generous severance packages in place, however, you will have the ability to act in the long-term interest of everyone.

We take a big chance with every person we hire. Our company has been inventing new ways to deliver information, developing new and more effective forms of direct marketing. That means we are also "inventing" new people to develop and carry out those programs. The fact that we are a team company, with all managers—even those who used to head whole departments in their previous jobs—doing hands-on work—makes each employee a vital element in the whole equation. If someone is out of step, out of rhythm, out of harmony with our fast-moving teams, we have big problems.

But letting people go disrupts their lives. I pledged to myself that I would do whatever I could to help terminated employees put their lives back together again.

Rarely can an individual do that in a week, or even a month. I try to give them the time they need to find another good job. If the person gets one before the end of the severance term we've provided, severance pay stops. But if he/she has been hustling to locate a new position and isn't successful in that already "unreasonable" length of time, we have given even more "unreasonable" extensions. I don't know of a single former employee who took unfair advantage of us.

Generous severance—what some would call unreasonable severance—works. In today's business atmosphere, a disgruntled former employee can be a loose cannon, causing irreparable harm to your company. Generosity at dismissal cuts that risk. At the same time, it unties your hands to make the tough personnel decisions necessary to keep your company running at peak performance.

"I" Power on firing

Management must take responsibility for its own flawed work—in hiring, training, supervising—and, of course, in providing enough work.

Habits are at first cobwebs, at last cables.

—English proverb

23. Putting Power Where It Is Needed Continuously

The improvement in systems and changes in responsibility generated by "I" Power sometimes eliminates jobs.

For instance, we recently did away with our one-person personnel department. The change was prompted by my own "I" Power suggestion in the form of a question: If we needed a personnel manager with 120 people—and a lot of turnover—do we really need one with 60 people and virtually no turnover?

The personnel manager moved over to editorial research, where her work is much more valuable to the company. Key aspects of the personnel job have been picked up by other people. All of them are enthusiastic about their added responsibilities. They are learning new skills, of course, and earning additional compensation.

To make change possible without hurting our people—if the change moves a person into a job with less complex responsibilities—we do not lower the salary. Sometimes we even give the person a raise for making the change.

This isn't prompted by pure altruism. We find that putting a more experienced person into what has been considered a less complicated job often results in constructive development of the job—and adds value to the company.

> **Use "I" Power to stay fluid and flexible in your approach to job placement**

That's the way to run lean and stay strong in today's competitive times.

James Harvey Robinson used to say that we rose from the ape because like him we kept 'monkeying around,' always meddling with everything about us. True, there is a difference, because, although the ape meddles, he forgets, and we have learned, first to meddle and remember, and then to meddle and record.

—Judge Learned Hand

24. Reviewing Your Reviews

Like a lot of standard business practices, performance reviews seem designed to encourage mediocrity and the status quo. Built-in mechanisms keep them that way. They are confrontational (if not overtly, then at least covertly). And they are rote. Employees and employers alike approach these reviews with distaste.

With "I" Power, we find that cooperation is always better than confrontation. Why, then, do many businesses persist in this empty exercise that pits the authority—the boss, the expert, the supervisor—against the next down the line—the accused, the examined, the subordinate?

Using "I" Power, you can turn the whole process around.

Twice a year our managers at Boardroom go over job descriptions of individuals in their departments. They fine-tune the specifications, since jobs are continually changing. They then give the revised descriptions to the individuals working in the jobs described. They ask the employees to make changes in the descriptions. Together, they also work out a ranking of the elements of the job, in descending order of importance.

The next step is the most important. It represents a true "I" Power innovation. We ask the employees to rank themselves.

This puts the performance review on a whole other footing from the confrontational mode to conventional business practice. It brings employees into the process from the beginning, encouraging them to review in their own minds how they could do their jobs better instead of preparing to defend how they perform now.

Managers go over these self-reviews, noting differences in how employees rate themselves and how the manager would rate them. Then the manager and the person being evaluated sit down to discuss these differences.

This is rarely a difficult conversation. The focus is always on ways to achieve personal growth through more effective work.

In the reviews that I do personally, I find that generally people judge themselves more harshly than I would have. That's constructive. They are setting higher and higher standards for their own performance.

Only occasionally do people grant themselves a too-favorable review. "I agree with you," I say in those few cases. "You are good, but I'm here to help you get better. Your review of yourself shows little room for improvement. So let's try a slightly different angle. Please rerate yourself against what you imagine to be the *world's best* at what you do."

Works like a charm.

"I" Power makes performance reviews more effective

The people being reviewed know their strengths and weaknesses and can do much to develop themselves if allowed, and encouraged, to do so.

The best compost for the lands
Is the wise master's feet and hands.

—Robert Herrick

25. Managing Yourself and Others by Priorities ...Not by Objectives

American business is keeping a deep, dark secret. One of its most cherished business techniques, management by objectives, is a fraud. From my observation, the hallowed technique has become more a management game than a management tool.

If you're locked into a management by objectives strategy, what is your natural impulse? If you're human, you try to set objectives low enough so you won't be embarrassed by not meeting them. Managers have been doing this for years in companies across the country, thereby institutionalizing mediocre performance instead of setting real objectives to raise quality and productivity.

This kind of cynicism leads to another conscious or unconscious deceit. Setting objectives becomes a sterile once- or twice-a-year exercise. Managers intuit what their objectives are "supposed to be," based on an overall company plan. Once their bosses are satisfied with the statements, the objectives statement is stashed in a desk drawer. The managers go about managing operations day to day, without giving the objectives much thought—until the next time the whole process begins again.

At Boardroom, we now manage not by objectives but by priorities. The apparatus we've developed to put this system into place is simple. Initially, I used it personally as a device to learn, think and focus as the challenges of running a growing business increased.

For years before developing what I call my Personal Priorities Form [see page 108], I had successfully used a personal journal to capture and sort out ideas and priorities. But keeping up the journal became more difficult as my job responsibilities, along with my personal life, became more and more complex. That's when I came up with this form to organize my own thinking.

I've used the form for years now as a kind of artificial intelligence—a way to get my own personal computer, my brain, to identify problems and generate solutions to those problems. And to create powerful new ideas, too.

By conventional measures, I believe my mind is only a modest-sized personal computer, but I have been able to accomplish and build some remarkable things by using this Priorities Form to organize my own thinking.

People who use computers always warn: Garbage in. Garbage out. And that holds true, too, for our minds. It's a challenge for each of us to fill our minds with useful information and to focus that information on things that really matter. So when I found the form working so well for me, I introduced it to the 20 or so key people at Boardroom who had the broadest responsibilities for keeping things running smoothly and healthily.

Each month, each of these key people lists on the form the most important opportunities opening up in the upcoming month and the problems to be solved during that month.

For each statement of opportunity or problem, they describe the action they plan to take that month.

At the same time, each of these people submits a copy of the Priority Form sent in the previous month. Next to each "Planned Action" noted on that form, they indicate the level of completion with a code:

- D—done.
- MA—moving along.
- HD—half done.
- DA—dragging along.
- ZD—zero done.
- P—problem.

There's a $5-per-day penalty for getting the forms in late. (Proceeds go to a local charity.)

For these key people, the Priorities Form has become a regular system—a system with deadlines—to review their own priorities, evaluate whether they still make sense and recognize whether they have or have not made progress in realizing the opportunities or solving the problems they identify.

For me the forms represent a timely, quick-glance system for reviewing their work. Anything that seems to need my personal attention becomes immediately apparent.

When someone is stalled, we sit down to talk through the situation and figure out what needs to be done to move it along. Sometimes, we can agree that another person who has more resources or time right then should tackle it.

This simple priorities system has been very effective in keeping our attention and energies focused on what needs to be done here at Boardroom. There's no place to hide, and no need to do so.

"I" Power supplies the ideas

Management By Priorities supplies the focus.

Priorities for January 1999

NAME _____   Department _____

OPPORTUNITIES

1. _____

    Planned action : _____
    _____
    _____
    _____

2. _____

    Planned action : _____
    _____
    _____
    _____

3. _____

    Planned action : _____
    _____
    _____
    _____

4. _____

    Planned action : _____
    _____
    _____
    _____

5. _____

    Planned action : _____
    _____
    _____

PROBLEMS

1. _____

    Planned action : _____
    _____
    _____
    _____

2. _____

    Planned action : _____
    _____
    _____
    _____

3. _____

    Planned action : _____
    _____
    _____
    _____

4. _____

    Planned action : _____
    _____
    _____
    _____

5. _____

    Planned action : _____
    _____
    _____

Said, done.

—Terence

26. It's Not Just Talent That Counts... How Talent Is Used Is Even More Important

Our business works best when each department head is also its very best worker. We work most productively that way, and produce the best-quality products.We expect managers to get their hands dirty—not just manage, but do the work of the department with the utmost skill.

Managers like this set the right example, so they are the perfect people to train others. They have realistic expectations about the pace of work in the department. Who better to monitor quality? Who better to make precise evaluations of people in the department? Hands-on managers are the natural conduits for "I" Power suggestions about improving the process of work.

Getting our hands dirty is the style right up to the top of the company. I participate in all editorial meetings. I edit copy, change layouts, write headlines and suggest improvements in our promotion pieces. Everything in the business is my business.

Sometimes, though, it is precisely because the department head is hands-on that we run into conflicts.

The most productive, creative, efficient worker—the department's boss, in other words—may hate the nitty-gritty details of administration. Things like keeping schedules, booking freelancers, or approving bills for payment. Does the boss want the no-win drudgery of supervising timeliness. No! How about making sure the department's working conditions—lights, temperature, enough wastebaskets, a better photocopier—are the best they can be?

Yet paying attention to these tasks makes the work of the department flow more easily.

MAKE THE ASSISTANT THE BOSS

"I" Power suggests a different method of *organizational* flow. Very often the person who can handle those details best is the boss's assistant.

I've seen the wisdom of this arrangement work so many times that I now make the assistant the "boss" with great confidence. In reality, what we create is a two-headed department that operates very efficiently.

One department head made the suggestion to me directly. "I love the creative side of my job," he said. "I'm very good at it. But I hate handling all the administrative details. Why don't we put Ms. Smith in charge of that?"

Since I believed the assistant was perfectly capable of doing the job, I talked to her immediately. She was willing to take over.

"Okay, I'm taking your suggestion," I told the department head. But I warned him that in many ways Ms. Smith was going to be "boss" of the department.

He looked very surprised.

"She'll be in charge of keeping the department schedules," I explained. "She'll be doing all the interfacing with others in the department, and those outside it. She'll be watching your productivity along with that of everyone else."

That startled him.

I assured him that if the new arrangement didn't work out, we would sit down and talk things through until we got them to work right.

The department ran beautifully for about a year, as he was able to focus on the creative work that he was so good at. Then I noticed, as did others around him, that he had been growing more aloof from other people in the department. He was even a bit sullen, which was a change from his usual behavior. So we had a talk. He confessed to me that though he enjoyed the ability to concentrate on his creative work, he found, to his surprise, that he resented being "out" of things in the department. He missed people asking his opinion—even questions about the administration of the department, which he used to hate having to deal with.

The next step was a three-way conversation—him, me and the person now handling administration of the department. Now that the subject was open, and his feelings were clear to the administrator, who had been trying (too effectively, it turned out) to spare him administrative details, the two easily worked out an arrangement for weekly meetings on what was taking place in the department, what administrative changes were under consideration, what "I" Power suggestions had been made and which should be implemented. He now contributes to the continuing improvement—and can still focus on his creative work.

NO WASTE OF TALENT

In other departments, the people at the top bury themselves in generating and improving the products their units supply for the company. They're craftsmen, and they do an excellent job. Meanwhile, their assistants keep things running right.

Crafting the particular product—in our company's business it just happens to be a publication—isn't the entire job. In many companies, talented people who love their work feel forced to trade away the practice of their craft in order to qualify for a promotion to head the unit. The penalty they pay is one that the company pays also. They wind up spending most of their time doing what they hate to do—administering details and supervising the work of others.

Our informal dual-head system avoids that waste of talent.

Will teaming up your department head's job add unnecessary compensation expense?

Not at all. All "bosses" are directly involved in the work at Boardroom. They are top-level people doing what they like to do and do best. They execute much of the work that in more traditional organizational structures is handled by less skilled, less motivated employees.

Each of these units now puts out quality products with half or less than half the number of staff people we had under a more conventional structure. That's a concrete, bottom-line saving, and "I" Power made the difference.

"I" Power gives you real power

You can toss out organizational hierarchies and assign work to people who can do it best, even if it means making the assistant the "boss."

The world is a mirror...Show yourself in it and it will reflect your image.

—Arabic proverb

27. Using "I" Power to Improve Your Reception

Most businesses have a somewhat impressive—and often costly—reception area. And they hire people to sit in that area and answer the phones on the basis of their looks—or their willingness to accept minimum wages in exchange for not having to do very much.

What a waste! How demoralizing!

These people make a major impact on company visitors and company callers...and most important of all, on company employees.

Most employees pass through the reception area several times a day. What impression do *they* draw about company priorities (let alone what visitors think) when the phone receptionist is usually reading a book, making personal calls, chatting with other employees hanging around the desk or just looking painfully bored?

We make sure this is one of the busiest areas in the company.

We staff it with people who smile on the phone when

113

they speak—no matter how busy the lines are—with people who can handle a variety of tasks and switch from one to the other without getting frazzled or *sounding* that way on the phone.

Some of the useful work they do:

• Open mail addressed to specific departments. This gives mail-room workers a hand so everyone's mail is distributed very quickly after the mail carrier drops off the sacks.

• Open envelopes for customer surveys and tally the responses.

• Measure the effectiveness and economies of various messenger and overnight delivery services. And make recommendations for change.

• Collate bills from delivery services. Check them for accuracy. Code them for the accounting department.

• Monitor the company fax machines, which are located here. Our front-office people call individuals to pick up their faxes as soon as they arrive.

Reception area workers are busy. We reward them generously for being able to handle a variety of chores. And for taking the initiative to work as a team and switch assignments as work loads change during the day or week.

We keep looking for tasks done in other parts of the company that the receptionist team can be trained to do. For instance, we used to hire an outside specialist to index our publications. Now our receptionists do it, moving to the computer in their area to continue the ongoing task whenever they can.

The goal is for people in the unit to see opportunities to earn more as they take on more skilled work—even though they continue to work right in that area. The company gets its reward, too: A pool of well-trained, active, competent employees.

To those within the company, as well as visitors, this

area *looks*—and *sounds* to outsiders who call in to the company—very different from the more typical scene: A bewildered phone receptionist with too many calls to answer and too little training to handle them gracefully. One who "drops" calls instead of transferring them...or neglects to monitor the board to see if callers are hanging on to silence.

Your reception area is your face to the world.

> ### Use "I" Power to help employees upgrade their own skills

They don't always need promotions to increase their value to the company and earn raises.

Do not put a sword into a madman's hand.

—English proverb

28. The Delegation Lie

Like many entrepreneurs, I was a hands-on, walk-around manager long before such behavior was applauded in trendy books about business and in the lecture halls of business schools. For me, it was a necessity.

But as Boardroom grew and I added talented and eager professionals and managers to our staff, the pressures on me to delegate increased. Consultants urged me to delegate. Experts we interviewed for articles in *Boardroom Reports* (now titled *Bottom Line/Business*) urged it, too. People who worked for me, whose performance I regarded highly, pushed more and more to call the shots themselves.

Finally, I gave in…with a vengeance. I moved my office from the central core of activity to another part of the floor—separated by a long corridor and a closed door. The goal, I told myself: Get people out of the habit of checking with me about details.

I had always been involved in even the minute detail

of planning mailings to add subscribers—the key marketing activity here. Now, with a growing staff, I had experienced professionals working for me who had planned successful mailings for some of the nation's biggest publishers. So I decided to let go of the reins.

In short order, and for the first time in Boardroom's existence, we got into a real financial bind. I learned my lesson fast…and in time to control the damage.

Delegation is a very high-risk alternative to hands-on management.

Only mediocrity can be delegated. High performance cannot be. High performance requires constant vigilance.

The potentially fatal traps for strong managers in delegating:

   • They dump rather than delegate—handing over task details they hate. *Result:* They lose control of the implementation.

   • They're so nervous and/or guilty about delegating that they try to turn over responsibility as quickly as possible. They fail to communicate clearly what they expect the outcome of the delegation to be—the goals that must be met and the deadlines. *Result:* The same as above.

The real alternative, the alternative that works all the time, is *continuous involvement of all employees at every level of the organization in the process of continuous improvement.*

When I needed a new way to manage because delegation failed and Boardroom had grown too big for hands-on management alone, "I" Power became the technique that worked.

Why "I" Power works better than delegation

It works from the bottom up, involving everyone in the organization, including those closest to both the work and the company's customers.

Except in poker, bridge and similar play-period activities, don't con anybody. Don't con yourself either.

—Robert Townsend

29. The Not-So-Secret Power of the "I" Power Meeting

There's no bigger time-waster in American companies than the ritualized weekly staff meetings in which everyone in a department or the managers of a division report on what they've been doing. Yet once our company started to grow, we drifted into just such formulaic meetings.

The impetus to change originated with our own top Executive Committee. We had endured the weekly staff meetings ourselves, and felt we needed a way to work more effectively.

We now meet weekly, from 4:30 to 5:30 on Tuesday one week and over lunch for a more expansive follow-up meeting the next week.

Each member contributes to the agenda. On Thursday, they give the Executive Committee coordinator forms with their suggested subjects to discuss at the next meeting. Copies of all the subjects proposed are distributed to every member of the Executive Committee. The coordinator goes over the forms on Friday and numbers the items for discussion by priority. That list is distributed on Monday as the agenda for the Tuesday meeting.

I review the final agenda right before the meeting and make any necessary adjustments. Attached to the agenda, as a trigger to thinking, are copies of each member's sheet. Of course, items can be added to the agenda even as the meeting progresses.

Our other teams are now adapting this technique to their weekly meetings. The big benefit has been that instead of wasting time with show-and-tell, we now can focus on the biggest opportunities and the biggest problems.

Working together, with everyone more aware of what's going on that's important throughout the company, our work has real focus. We solve problems intelligently and quickly. When opportunity knocks, we are always mobilized to answer, because this system forces a discussion of opportunities.

The No Secrets "I" Power meetings

The people who come to the meeting make the agenda.

No one is great enough or wise enough for any of us to surrender our destiny to. The only way in which anyone can lead us is to restore to us the belief in our own guidance.

—Henry Miller

30. Team Power Beats Managerial Excellence

By accident—and as a direct result of "I" Power—I discovered early in our "I" Power adventure that managers are far less important to getting excellent performance out of a department team than most business professors, consultants or senior or junior managers realize, or imagine, or are ready to acknowledge.

At the time I made this discovery, I was frustrated in working with a leading recruiter to find a manager to head a critically important department of the company.

There had been an unprecedented series of disruptive changes at the top of this department within a short period of time.

The first department head, who had been with the company from its earliest, simplest days, decided to leave when the unit's operations became big and complex. The next head, recruited from a much bigger firm, resigned after a couple of years to work for an even bigger firm. The third head, promoted from within, moved farther out to the suburbs, finally decided that the long commute to Manhattan took too much time away from family responsibilities—and resigned to work as a consultant. Another key person in the department left to take care of an ailing parent in another part of the country.

At that point I put the second in command of the department in charge, someone who was new to the company. But I made it clear that the move was only temporary and that I would be interviewing candidates for the top job from outside the company. My concern was that this new person did not have much experience in managing people or our special systems.

By that time, we had already started "I" Power in its initial form—asking people at every meeting to come up with three suggestions for improving operations. Results were already so encouraging that I asked the temporary department head to focus "I" Power on the work of his department.

THE PERFORMANCE MACHINE

He began holding weekly meetings—they took only about half an hour—at which each person in the department was asked to come up with at least three suggestions on how to improve department operations. The suggestions were written down and reviewed.

Meanwhile, the search for a new manager from the outside dragged on and on. No candidate had enough specialized industry knowledge to provide something that we didn't already have. Or their personalities didn't fit.

Every week, however, the department staff continued to come up with at least ten ideas on how to improve its performance, how to simplify processes, how to operate more accurately and more quickly. And—they successfully followed through and implemented most of them.

Then one day I was having lunch with an outside consultant who worked closely with this department. "You know," he said to me, "you have the best performing department of its kind of any of our clients. And they are the most cooperative group that I work with." I replied that I had been thinking the same thing—and really appreciated his comparison. I hadn't been able to believe that they could be performing as well as it seemed they were doing. But it had turned out that they were.

That's the day I put an end to our search for a *new* department manager.

NO MORE MANAGEMENT STARS

The temporary head became the permanent head. The company continues to get excellent results with a person of satisfactory—but not outstanding—experience at the top...*plus* the thoughtful involvement of every department member (also light in experience) in continually improving the day-to-day processing of work.

Now—almost 1,500 ideas later—the group still regularly finds significant ways to improve its operations.

Your company, too, doesn't need management stars and heroes to thrive.

What it absolutely *does* need is an effective system for getting and implementing ideas from the people who do the work.

> **Intensify the use of "I" Power in problem departments**

You'll do better than you would with management heroes.

The superior man always remembers how he was punished for his mistakes. The inferior man always remembers what presents he got.

—Confucius

31. Business War Crime Paying Executives Too Much

Financial incentives for managers are wildly overrated in the US as the key way to improving company performance.

Top managements of many American companies spend far too much time working out complex compensation schemes and perks to enrich senior executives. They say they pay executives so much because every other company does the same. They have to stay competitive in high salaries and bonuses in order to attract the managers they need for the company to perform.

So they say.

They're wrong—if they really believe what they say. But chances are they *don't* really believe it. The rationale is simply a convenient cover for greed.

There is a story about one of the top compensation experts in the US—who is at the top because the top executives of the nation's top corporations pay him the most money to create compensation plans that will give *them* the most money. He is said to have commented: *Sometimes I wonder whether I'm a compensation consultant or a dentist. The whole business is caps, caps, caps, caps.*

What this intelligent, able man was saying was that he was a whore for management. They pay him to create satisfaction through fiction.

He knows and *they* know that the complex incentive systems he sets up are not really incentive systems.

Fiction: The plan sets a base salary—with performance bonuses for the executive if he/she meets this, that or the other goal.

Reality: The manager can easily reach the goal.

Dreaming up these fabrications is disgusting work. But for decades, that's how this brilliant man has been asked to apply his vast knowledge and intelligence. He was never asked to put those capacities to work to make companies more competitive—and more productive.

THE BIGGEST GAP

Top managers know full well what's going on. But they sit on one another's boards and they all go along with the fiction that fills their pockets.

In fact, it's clear by now that one of the key reasons American companies don't work better is that they have the biggest gap between the money paid to executives at the top and that earned by employees in the lowest ranks. That sets the example for the most talented workers. They go off and start their own ventures to be able to set up the same compensation schemes.

The situation is quite different in most Japanese companies. Top managers there average only 16 times the amount paid the workers at the bottom—instead of hundreds of times, as in many top US companies. And that doesn't handicap Japanese performance.

Myth: Managers respond only to financial rewards.

Reality: The best managers love the *process* of work as well as—sometimes even *more* than—achieving monetary goals.

Even after reaching a goal, the best managers—in fact, the best employees *right down the line*—keep trying to find an even better way.

COMPENSATION MYTHS

Myth: Compensation systems can be so cunningly designed that, like heat-seeking missiles, they lead managers directly to the company's tactical and strategic targets.

Reality: The executives on a financial incentive plan spend more time figuring out how to "work the system" to maximize their personal incentive bonuses than on getting the company's systems to work better.

Myth: Goal-directed managers are the chief reason companies improve their performance. *Reality:* Lower-paid workers in any company have far more stake in how well the company performs than most managers realize. Most of these workers invest—or are willing to invest—their lives in the company. They often stay at the same job or same level for *decades.* Managers often move on—and on—before the wreckage of their short-term opportunism or incompetence surfaces.

Given an opportunity to contribute ideas through a program such as "I" Power, the workers will startle themselves—and most managers—with their knowledge of how to get top quality and top efficiency out of company operations.

The "I" Power compensation scheme

Greater security and satisfaction from improving the way the organization works—continually.

The most practical advice for leaders is not to treat pawns like pawns, nor princes like princes, but all persons like persons.

—James MacGregor Burns

32. The Compensation Conundrum
A Fairness Puzzle

For years I tried to come up with a compensation system that would provide real incentives for excellence. I wanted one that would not lock the company into paying for mediocrity or entice our people to work the system for bonuses, endangering our overall team efforts.

I read everything I could find on the subject. Over the years I've talked with more than a dozen of the top experts on compensation, hoping to uncover secrets that worked. Most of all, I've analyzed for myself the pros and cons of various compensation and incentive systems.

In my experience, incentives seem to work in most sales situations—not perfectly all the time, but at least much of the time. Properly structured incentive pay can work in piecework operations, I believe, as long as there are rewards for quality output and penalties for flaws.

But for our editorial work, direct marketing, accounting and other office systems, incentives don't seem to be at all applicable.

One of my responses to this puzzle is to keep Boardroom salaries ahead of the market (at least my sense of the market). That has worked to attract and keep able people.

Then, to help our people feel good about continuing their efforts toward personal improvement and cutting costs, we initiated a profit-sharing arrangement around the same time "I" Power was introduced.

Unfortunately, the peculiarities of our particular business make it difficult, if not impossible, to have a clear-cut statement of profits, except for IRS purposes. What satisfies the tax authorities doesn't satisfy me as a good measure of the success of our people's efforts, however.

In good times, we demand the most from people because we invest more heavily in promotion and have to plan and implement more mailings. That reduces rather than increases our short-term profits. Just the opposite happens in bad times. When we can, we cut down on promotion and mailings, but our cash flow continues.

I now accept the fact that no formula works as well as common sense and an honest effort to be fair.

Each quarter, I review what we've done together and come up with a figure to distribute as a share of profits. I bring that figure—so far not less than ten percent of total salaries annually—to our Executive Committee and we discuss it.

Share of profits is pegged to salary, represented as a percentage of the whole payroll. If an employee's salary is 1 percent of the payroll, say, then the share of profits is the same 1 percent slice of the pie. If we have reason to explain why the lump sum of profits to be shared isn't greater, we do.

In particular, I go to great pains to make it clear that there's nothing automatic about this distribution. The funds that make it possible have to be generated by increasingly effective work by all of us. My conclusion is that fair compensation is really not as hard to arrive at as some experts would have us believe. The key is honestly trying to be fair.

We adjust individuals' salaries, of course, as continuing change increases their responsibilities.

The result of this overall compensation approach is that we have lost only one person that I know of because of money through the years. That was an odd situation. A Wall Street firm in the middle of an emergency offered our person more than double an already fair salary. But that emergency didn't last very long—and neither did the job.

THE FAIRNESS PUZZLE

There are still problems of fairness in compensation that puzzle me. Boardroom operated in the high-cost New York metropolitan area. Our salary levels recognized this reality. Since we run a profitable business, I have no problem with generous compensation, if giving even the lowest paid people in our company enough money to live with dignity in an expensive community can be called being generous.

But if two people are doing virtually the same job at the same level of competence and intelligence for the same compensation, is it "fair" when one of them is a single parent supporting three young children, or is responsible for aged parents, and the other is either single with no other financial responsibilities or part of a dual-income household? The law says it is fair. Frankly, I'm not sure.

The solution involves that old demon of corporate bureaucracies, flexibility—a very important "I" Power trait. When special personal problems arise for people in our company, we are very quick to be helpful in any way that we can. That, of course, includes being financially helpful.

Consideration of the "fairness puzzle" has even affected my thinking about the important inspirational art collection, "Lessons in Life," that I have built. The collection has been a real inspiration to all of us at Boardroom and to many others as pieces from it are shown in museums around the world.

As the collection grew, however, I found myself growing increasingly pained instead of proud. I concluded that there were far more important things for me to do in life than collect art. High in priority among those things I could do was to help my people live decently. Through "I" Power, I found a way to try to communicate the principles I had learned.

Two ways to face the Compensation Conundrum

Use common-sense profit sharing to unite your company rather than divisive pay scales that separate executives from workers. Be flexible and generous when it comes to meeting the special needs of your employees.

Successful generals make plans to fit circumstances, but do not try to create circumstances to fit plans.
—General George S. Patton, Jr.

33. Your "I" Power Plan For the Future

At Boardroom, we did a five-year plan, the first one in our 20 years of doing business. Making a five-year plan originated as an "I" Power suggestion. Now we update it every year—another "I" Power suggestion.

We really had not needed a plan during many years of successful growth. We'd been very busy with more projects than we could handle. By now, however, our mix of editorial products is pretty much under control. We know how to get them out efficiently. We know how to market them effectively. Thanks to "I" Power, we have even more new ideas now, by far, than ever before.

It was time to look ahead to see what else we wanted to do.

I had not pushed for long-term planning through the years, chiefly because I recalled what the head of strategic planning for one of the world's leading consulting firms told me years ago: Those in any business who think they can effectively plan more than nine months ahead are crazy.

The Japanese have proven him wrong, however. Some of their companies don't stop at five- or even ten-year plans. Some of them have 100-year company plans!

Our own planning started with general discussions in our Executive Committee. The members wrote statements of where they would like the company to be in five years. As it turned out, the objectives were all quite similar, and it didn't take me long to review and combine them into a five-year look-ahead.

Our plans for the future are relatively modest. We have no great need to create a lot of new products. Our current ones show every sign of being able to grow significantly. We've already identified "buds" on each of our publications that are likely to flower into new ways to serve our customers. So we expect our product line as well as sales of our current products to double in five years. If that rate of growth doesn't happen, we will still be very much okay.

Right now we have a sales/employee ratio that's higher by far than that of any Fortune 500 company. Forced growth beyond what we project would only push us into debt. Directly or indirectly, we could wind up with bankers or other lenders running our business. Ugh!

Our Executive Committee had previously agreed that we didn't want the company to go public. Being public puts unreasonable strains and restraints on operations. The chief benefit of going public, as we see it, goes to the principal stockholders, who get a lot of cash.

We won't be big, but we will be doing what we like to do and what we do best. Good things for people...good things for America—and the world. To be able to continue doing it all well in the increasingly tricky times ahead means that we have to work continually to do things better and better.

"I" Power and your five-year plan

Get company-wide input into the plan. Shared goals are tremendously effective. Imposed goals rarely are.

Lay down the most complicated movements intelligibly, but in a few words—with simplicity.

—Napoleon

34. It's Simple But Not Easy

We've been saying all along that it's simple to unlock the ideas and motivation of the people who work in your organization—and to put their ideas to work.

But simple does not mean *easy*.

Managers can cut off the valuable flow of enthusiasm and ideas…

> •…by careless inattention to details.
> •…by failing to respond *immediately*.
> •…by not taking *all* ideas seriously.
> •…by simply saying "No."
> •…by criticizing a suggestion without giving the person who contributed the idea a chance to explain further, add details and respond to questions.
> •…by not probing for ideas—*insisting* on ideas for processing work better—at every regular department meeting.

And most destructive of all, managers guarantee

137

failure by making the idea-generating process a low-level, bureaucratic function rather than a *major responsibility of the top person in charge.*

It takes valuable input—*your* time, *your* thought, *your* dedication—to get valuable output. But it's output that you will not achieve in any other way—no matter how hard *you* worked at it yourself.

> **The "I" in "I" Power is *you***

The New Weapons of
The New War

35. The New Weapons of The New War

As we've said, there's nothing complicated about putting the ideas in this book to work for you immediately.

To get you started right away, you might find it useful to adapt some of the forms that Boardroom has developed over the last couple of years to make "I" Power work smoothly.

So, send for a free kit of "I" Power forms.

Write to:

> "I" Power Forms
> Greenwich Institute for American Education
> 55 Railroad Ave.
> Greenwich, CT 06830

The Kit Includes:

1. "I" Power suggestion form—and code for rating ideas.
2. Sample reward envelope.
3. Sample "I" Power Report and "I" Power Accomplish-

ments Report, as an example of how to report ideas and progress on implementation to all employees.

4. Priorities Report—for keeping yourself and your managers focused on the chief problems to be solved and the top opportunities to develop.

For information about "I" Power Training Seminars, write to:

> Greenwich Institute for American Education
> 55 Railroad Ave.
> Greenwich, CT 06830

Or call:

> 1-800-625-2424/203-625-5920.

We Want to Hear From You

36. We Want to Hear From You

Anything can be done better than the way it's being done now. So we want to hear about your own experiences with using "I" Power in your organization. (The free "I" Power forms offered on page 141 will help.)

Let us know, by fax or mail, how "I" Power works for you.

Martin Edelston
Boardroom, Inc.
55 Railroad Ave.
Greenwich, CT 06830
Fax: 203-861-7057

What unusual problems did you face? Did you solve them? How? Have you made useful adaptations?

Are you stuck?

We're prepared to work together to make this battle plan victorious.

Real Questions
Real Ideas

Most people make the mistake of planning only on the basis of what they know. The trick is to lay what you do know against all there is to know, make the subtraction and then try to find out as much as possible of the needed-to-know unknown.

—William Safire

37. "I" Power Questions To Provoke Useful Ideas at Meetings

These questions are being used successfully at Boardroom meetings...

☐ How can I be more efficient at my job?

☐ How can my department be more efficient?

☐ What would I do (or not do) differently if I were president of this company?

☐ What can I personally do to reduce costs next year without affecting quality?

☐ What can my department do to reduce costs next year without affecting quality?

☐ What can the company do to reduce costs next year without affecting quality?

☐ What's my pet business peeve?

☐ What simple thing can I do to be much more effective at work?

☐ What is holding me back from being much, much more effective at work?

☐ Three things I would like to accomplish in the coming year.

☐ One thing I'd like my department/company to accomplish in the coming year.

☐ What can I do to cut costs or increase business?

☐ What can my department do to cut costs or increase business?

☐ What can our company do to cut costs or increase business?

☐ How can we improve the "I" Power program?

☐ How are we "shooting ourselves in the foot?" (What costly mistakes are we making?)

☐ Best way I know of that we can cut costs.

☐ Best way I can think of to increase sales.

☐ With half of the year gone, what is the most important professional goal I want to attain by year end?

☐ What is my number-two goal?

☐ What is my number-three goal?

☐ What should the company try to achieve by year-end?

☐ What is the biggest mistake I made in the past six months, and what did I learn from it?

☐ What is my single best achievement of the past six months?

☐ What's the one thing I, as an employee, could do to improve Boardroom?

☐ What's the one thing that Boardroom, as a company, could do to make my job more productive?

☐ Each employee could submit a story idea he/she would love to see in a publication and explain why.

☐ What changes in different departments could be made to speed up production?

☐ What would I do to help a department I work with closely to increase output?

☐ Start with groups of two, three or four people who interact with one another regularly. Seat them together at lunch. Have them come up with ideas on how their areas could work together better. Report the best ideas to the whole group during dessert.

☐ What can we do to improve communication in the company?

☐ How can my department communicate better with top management?

☐ How can we relieve stress in this workplace?

☐ Without worrying about costs, what outside influence/machine/computer would you want to enhance your personal effectiveness?

☐ How could my supervisor supervise better?

☐ What is Boardroom missing? What does it need to be perfect for you?

☐ What can we do to strengthen the communication among departments?

☐ What is most important to you in business?

☐ What can the company do to improve long-range planning?

☐ When I make a decision that impacts other departments and/or personnel, how do I alert them to the change?

☐ How much time do I waste with personal phone calls and lengthy chitchat?

☐ How much of an expenditure should Boardroom be making in research and development?

☐ What would I like to see more of in Boardroom's publications?

☐ What would I like to see less of in Boardroom's publications?

☐ An idea for a new marketing procedure or product department.

☐ In what new direction would I like to see my department move?

☐ What is the one thing I must do at work that I feel is no longer necessary or effective?

☐ With the high cost of health care today, what can we do as a company to ensure that we continue with our current protection—or make it better—without incurring too much expense?

☐ What plans or preparations do we need to make in order to ensure that the company performs at an optimum level during the next five years?

☐ Where do you see the company in the next five years...accomplishments, new products, etc?

☐ What can I do to improve my present surroundings in terms of safety?

☐ What do I personally need to learn or do to prepare to meet the new demands that lie ahead?

☐ What can my department do to communicate better with other departments? What can other departments do to communicate better with my department?

☐ What three things can I best implement in order to become better organized...accomplish more in less time?

☐ What is the mission statement of my department?

☐ What can we learn from other companies?

☐ What is most important to me here at Boardroom?

☐ How can we institute more continuous job training?

☐ How can I personally use "I" Power to improve/benefit myself?

☐ How can I personally use "I" Power to improve/benefit my department?

☐ How can I personally use "I" Power to improve/benefit Boardroom?

☐ What changes should Boardroom make to better service our customers?

☐ What changes can my department make to better service our customers?

☐ What changes can I personally make to better service our customers?

☐ If I were the president of the company, what would I do in addition to what is already being done?

☐ What do you feel Boardroom's top three priorities should be? What do you think they are?

☐ What can I do to help fulfill the company's priorities?

☐ What can I do to keep my department focused on our long-term goals?

☐ What do I think would be a very profitable thing for the company to consider taking on?

☐ What would I like to see changed in the company to help it run more smoothly and efficiently?

☐ What would make "I" Power more powerful?

☐ What are my short-term goals for my department?

☐ What are my long-term goals for my department?

☐ What can I do to improve the quality of the work my department produces?

☐ What would I like to see done in another department to help my department run more efficiently?

☐ What have I accomplished in the last six months?

☐ In what three ways has "I" Power helped my department to become more efficient?

☐ What do I feel is excess baggage here?

☐ What do I want to be able to learn that I don't already know?

☐ How do I want my job to grow?

☐ If I could change one thing about my job, what would it be?

☐ If I could change one thing about my department, what would it be?

☐ If I could change one thing about the company, what would it be?

The best way to have a good idea is to have a lot of ideas.

—Dr. Linus Pauling

38. "I" Power Ideas
A Sampling of Recent Ideas Generated at Boardroom to Help Stimulate Your Thinking

ACCOUNTING

☐ Schedule specific days to do the first half and the end of the month's work.

☐ List all the reports that are needed for accounts receivable month-end reports.

☐ Time to advise our bank to reconsider charging us for the return of customers' bad checks.

☐ When bills come in from vendors, always check them before submitting them to accounting.

COMMUNICATION

☐ When communication problems come up—stop and ask, "What can I do to be clearer?"

☐ At meetings, when ideas and/or tasks surface, someone should be delegated to jot down information.

☐ Encourage callers to use direct-dial numbers.

COMPUTERS/TECHNOLOGY

☐ Install two different packages of Virus Protection Software on all computers.

☐ In addition to Hard Disk Utilities loaded on all computers, create emergency start-up disk with volume (hard disk) data for each computer.

☐ Secure selected (Accounting, Executive Committee, Purchasing) computers with security software.

☐ Purchase additional Multisync monitors for back-up on PCs and Macs.

☐ Purchase external floppy drives and hard drives for back-up on PCs and Macs.

☐ Two monthly tape archives will be created, one for the department and one for the vault.

☐ Schedule monthly meeting with each department to discuss pros and cons of computer operations.

☐ Purchase portable computers for back-up and off-site production.

☐ Record all software and hardware errors and distribute quarterly to each related computer user.

☐ Allow flexibility in computer setup (hardware and software) as long as compatibility is sustained. Do not expect every employee to work the same.

CUSTOMER SERVICE

☐ Make everyone in the company aware of the lifetime value of a customer and the cost of replacing one.

☐ Show employees our service guarantees to remind them that it's everyone's goal to provide good service.

☐ Can we try a new way to say thanks to our customers? Each month, or every few months, we can have a business-card drawing.

☐ We need to hold more meetings that focus on identifying what our customers want and need.

☐ Since we are creating new product-development teams, let's do a survey of buyers of our products to find out what they like about our existing products and what they would like to see developed.

☐ Send a duplicate premium immediately upon receiving a customer complaint rather than sending a letter that simply creates problems.

☐ Before changes are made in our phone/customer-relations policy, we should poll other publications for their methods. This may give us a feel for the industry standard and help us to excel in this area, too.

☐ For bills that are more than 60 days past due, look into the possibility of sending a follow-up past-due invoice.

☐ From time to time, have someone order products from competitors to see what they are doing and how long it takes them to respond.

☐ If we find ourselves saying "no" to a customer, we must explore why we are not able to reply "yes."

☐ Allow customers who are installment buyers and pay in full on first bill to buy more than one book on "Bill Me" basis.

☐ Try calling customers at random and asking them about any problems.

EDITORIAL

☐ Consider asking *Bottom Line/Personal* readers to submit money-saving ideas they've been implementing throughout the recession.

☐ Consider a monthly nutrition column in *Bottom*

Line/Health similar to the one in *The New York Times.*

☐ When editing or copyediting *Bottom Line* stories, make the effort to flag any statements that sound suspicious or need to be fact-checked further.

☐ Return edited stories to writers so they can see what was done to the original.

☐ Consider a panel of experts for each publication.

☐ It is very important that all subjects in our books be updated...not just the tax information.

☐ Production editors should flag stories that need a specific type of checking by marking "do geography check" and "do price check."

☐ Do positive, uplifting, continuous-improvement-illustrating cartoons in *Bottom Line/Business.*

☐ For all new freelance writers, we should send them a checklist of things needed in each story plus seven or so back issues so they are familiar with our style.

☐ Ask *Bottom Line*'s gardening expert to submit cut-off dates on when stories need to appear so they are published in the appropriate season and won't have to be held till next year or be killed.

☐ Offer an incentive for *Bottom Line* subscribers to send in story ideas.

☐ Hire freelance travel, health and banking experts to review the articles in the books.

☐ Publish a tax fact sheet as a supplement to *Tax Hotline.*

☐ To avoid last-minute fact-checking, when taking an author's correction, make it a point to double-check the information in the footnotes.

☐ Send formal letters to freelancers reminding them to get fax numbers and addresses for sources.

☐ Compile a list of the names, addresses, phone and fax numbers for everyone on our panel of experts.

☐ When choosing short quotes for *Bottom Line*, use lots of quotes from the Bible.

☐ Prepare a *Bottom Line* index.

☐ Publish a two-page supplement to *Tax Hotline* of home improvements that reduce the taxable gain when you sell your house.

☐ On any paperwork—manuscripts, memos, etc.— where more than one person is likely to scrawl comments, each of us should have one discrete color pen, and use it exclusively, so we'll always know who is saying what.

"I" POWER IMPROVEMENTS

☐ Have a theme each month in the "I" Power system.

☐ Ask that everyone make an "I" Power appointment with themselves each day so that the process becomes a good habit.

☐ When an "I" Power idea needs input or reaction from people in the organization, have someone on the "I" Power team meet with those people immediately.

☐ Before submitting an "I" Power suggestion about someone else, talk to them first so they know what is going on.

☐ For every two "I" Power ideas you come up with for others to do, come up with one for yourself.

☐ Consider getting "I" Power binders for all employees. Dividers could be made for "pending," "let's discuss," "action taken" and "accomplishments."

☐ Send out a list showing how everyone is doing on "I" Power.

☐ A company that is collaborating with us on our data base has a very extensive improvement system. Compare our system with theirs.

☐ Encourage everyone not to hide behind the "I" Power system. If something is an urgent need, take action to get it done instead of making a passive suggestion.

☐ In order to keep "I" Power goals clear, suggest a yearly total of quality ideas—to be evaluated semi-annually.

☐ Change "I" Power so that ideas are submitted directly to the concerned people, with a "cc" to "I" Power.

☐ To improve "I" Power, a form should be made up so that when a suggestion needs more of an explanation it can be given quickly, easily and in a well-organized fashion.

☐ We should keep a log of the "I" Power ideas that we submit.

MONEY-SAVING/COST-CUTTING

☐ Systematically review all vendors for service and price competitiveness.

☐ Try harder to consolidate printing jobs to increase quantities and lower prices.

☐ To keep us from again having "too much fat," a committee could be set up to determine the ideal number of employees in each department.

☐ Have a representative from Con Edison meet with us to discuss how we can make our operations more energy-efficient.

☐ Reduce the cost of insert ads in publications by bidding with several printers against our contract price.

☐ Make use of the Boardroom art collection in some way that is profitable to Boardroom.

☐ Negotiate with vendors to give us a price reduction if we pay invoices within ten days.

☐ Donate excess inventories to charities.

☐ Make it a policy to return toner cartridges from laser printers to Hewlett Packard for recycling.

☐ Before changing the ink cartridge on the new printers, use the prime button: The problem may be lack of fluid pressure, not lack of ink.

☐ If we use lighter packaging, we should be able to send the new *Tax Hotline* business premiums in a single package rather than send the calculator and book separately.

☐ If personal pads are redesigned, consider removing titles; this way, we can still use the pads if titles change.

☐ Annually update the medical-benefit status of our staff during the year...marital changes, children no longer eligible for coverage, etc.

☐ Look into a fax processing unit. The unit is linked to our PCs and can cut our phone bills a ton.

NEW PRODUCTS

☐ Produce Boardroom Books on cassette.

☐ Create a series of soft-cover supplements to Boardroom Books called "More..." (e.g., *More Inside Information, More Estate Planning*) and sell them to buyers of those titles.

☐ Develop a new book or premium on the subject of careers.

☐ Suggestion for a *Bottom Line/Health* premium— reprint *Bottom Line/Personal* psychology/self-help articles.

☐ Create a do-it-yourself living trust kit.

☐ Sell binders for our newsletters.

☐ Create a Boardroom-type book for young people.

☐ Adapt *Bottom Line* for use in secondary schools.

☐ Premium idea: Good health 365 times a year. A calendar-type book with a good-for-you tip each day.

OFFICE SERVICES/ADMINISTRATION

☐ To protect phone lines from going down, install two inbound lines from several different long-distance carriers. If one major carrier goes down, we'll have others to use as backup.

☐ Look into protecting our incoming calls with an AT&T 800 WATS line.

☐ To avoid accidents, have Office Services regularly check all telephone lines, extension cords and any electrical lines.

☐ Create a master company-wide calendar where people can write in meetings, dates, vacation, etc.

☐ In the book department, put up an erasable magnetic bulletin board to keep track of the upcoming week's projects.

☐ Clean the filters in the air conditioners regularly.

☐ Vendors, freelancers, consultants and contributing editors that Boardroom frequently does business with should receive a copy of our company phone list with all pertinent extensions circled.

☐ Have a telltale light or signal that lets us know when backup batteries on locks and computers are on.

☐ When sending FedEx packages, use the proper size envelopes for documents.

☐ If you must eat in your office due to an overload of paperwork/work on the computer, make a place for lunch as far away from the computer as possible.

☐ Give the computer manager a workbench area to work on equipment.

☐ Replace the glass shelves in the ladies' room for

safety reasons.

☐ When ordering lunch over the telephone, give your extension so the receptionist can call you.

PERSONNEL

☐ Implement a Job Evaluation Committee to oversee employee development.

☐ Create an evaluation system for subordinates to rate managers. This would help managers and subordinates to grow and understand one another better.

☐ Conduct a company-wide survey of how we feel about our benefits package.

☐ For new employees: In addition to our normal training techniques, write up a list of questions about their jobs and have them ask around to find the answers, to learn on their own and get to know colleagues.

☐ If a team member is changing vacation dates, it is important to tell Administration.

☐ The Personnel Committee should update policies on freelancers.

☐ When changing a department's procedures, the change should be documented so an individual can go back months later to review it.

☐ Recent experience with a transit strike has made it advisable that employees think of an alternate plan for getting to work.

☐ Have the entire team write a list of small clerical jobs they cannot get around to doing.

☐ Start an employee book club to encourage reading of developmental books.

☐ Self-health-care lessons to lessen our medical costs.

☐ Look into self-insuring group dental benefits vs. paying insurance-company monthly premiums and having them pay claims. No additional cost to us and some of the restrictions set by insurance company removed.

☐ Acquaint all staffers with all the different reference materials available to them.

☐ Have the Personnel Coordinator solicit suggestions from the staff on improving performance-review forms and procedures.

QUALITY IMPROVEMENT

☐ Anytime a new program is being developed, make a list of where it can go wrong so we can identify and avoid all risks.

☐ Have each of us submit at least one idea on how we feel a certain publication can be improved.

☐ Due to certain problems with printers bulk packing our materials, causing spoilage, we have provided our printers with a specific packing instruction sheet.

☐ Have a backup book printer for our main printer: They are good, but not for quick turnarounds.

☐ Look into "at-home dates" for delivery of third-class mail. We have been experiencing poor delivery times and "at-home dates" ensure delivery times.

☐ All overnight proofreaders should double-check their spelling corrections with the *Merriam-Webster's New Collegiate* dictionary before indicating them on their reads.

☐ In the future, we must do a trial run on anything we do that involves the customer.

☐ Replace the teeny-tiny "Timely report/please expedite" rubber stamp on the back covers of *Bottom Line/Business* and *Bottom Line/Personal* with a more convincing presentation of the same words.

☐ The next time the *Bottom Line* index is published,

highlight on the front cover that the index is there.

☐ Check samples of insert cards for publications immediately upon receipt so that there are no printing errors in those that go out.

☐ Idea for brainstorming meeting: Go through 24 issues of *Bottom Line/Business* or *Bottom Line/Personal*...pick the three we're most proud of. Then critique those for ways we could have done better.

SALES/MARKETING INNOVATIONS

☐ Issue wrap for *Bottom Line/Business* subscriber survey asking about editorial preferences, number of employees, titles, owner/partner, company functions, industry, etc.

☐ Start having creative meetings for billing and renewal series, and bring in outside people.

☐ Consider marketing our books on a CD-ROM disc.

☐ Look into placing space ads for selected books.

☐ Do a couple of price tests in Canada.

☐ When we promote to acquire new subscribers, we should be setting realistic goals to renew them.

☐ Consider celebrating Boardroom's 25th birthday by sending freebie "invite" to customers who have made two-plus Boardroom purchases, offering them a six-month free subscription to any other newsletter.

☐ Send a special mailing to older *Bottom Line* subscriptions that have expired with offer to try us again.

☐ When we mail our publications, we should insert promotions for our other products.

☐ Offer a cassette instead of a printed book as an alternative for our smaller premiums.

☐ Do a Father's Day promotion for books.

☐ Boost *Bottom Line/Health* renewals with an added

renewal bonus: A 4 × 6-inch laminated card suitable for keeping in one's kitchen...with the new basic food groups on one side and the latest suggested daily servings of each on the other.

☐ Time to think about a real big push on Christmas gift promo for our books.

☐ When mailing out *Healing Unlimited* we should consider inserting a current issue of *Bottom Line/Health* with promo as an incentive.

☐ If we could control the timing of tests in cold mail packages, we could save money by consolidating them on the end of controls and paying the lower price per thousand for printing.

☐ Consider "Canadianizing" *The Book of Secrets*—at least revise it to get rid of obvious US-only material.

☐ Reprints: Would it be possible to mail our book catalog out with them?

☐ Offer incentives to folks who get friends and acquaintances to subscribe.

☐ When we send our sources their complimentary issues of the publication their story appears in, enclose an offer card for three free issues to friends and associates of our sources.

☐ Test a larger bind-in card so that it can be folded and sealed. Makes it easier on people who pay by credit.

SECURITY

☐ Retain a computer-security consultant to conduct tracking tests.

☐ Consider putting a video camera in the mail room by the freight elevator.

☐ Tighten computer-identification card and password entry system.

☐ Check and chain down all valuable equipment.

SUPPLIERS

☐ Conduct a seminar with sales reps. They know what customers want, and that would be good for planning our direct-mail promotion.

☐ Put all of our major suppliers on as freebies for our publications.

☐ The purchasing department should put together a book of film specifications for all of our printers.

☐ Develop partnership agreements with outside vendors that formally make both parties accountable for performance measures.

TIME MANAGEMENT/EFFICIENCY/PRODUCTIVITY/ SHREWD THINKING

☐ Have team members use a daily sheet to help prioritize their daily tasks.

☐ If you have a group of similar documents or spread-sheets for different products, rename them so they will be grouped together logically by function in the computer.

☐ When someone is showing you an infrequently used procedure, take notes so you don't have to ask again.

☐ Each book, each premium, each reprint and original printing should have a book plan on how it will be printed, where it will be printed and the total cost, including typesetting, art, etc.

☐ Follow up on our recent *Bottom Line* editorial research: What actions have we taken as a result? What else should we be doing?

☐ Start a product-development team.

☐ Give one another closed door time—cover one another's phones.

□ Place an "in use" card/folder in the file cabinet report drawers to use when someone takes out a report to look at so that others will know that it is in use rather than lost or thrown out.

□ Hold strategy meetings for each product.

□ Train people in different departments so they can be helpful when needed.

□ Continually urge team members to notice things they have to do more than once.

How
Anheuser-Busch
Baxter Healthcare
Kodak
Do It

39. America Is Waking Up

In a surprising number of plants and offices across the US, a quiet revolution is taking place.

A cross section of the American work force—seasoned managers and long-time union workers, high-school and college graduates and dropouts all holding their first factory jobs, ex–ski bums, engineers and barely literate ex-farmhands—are increasing their productivity by using the methods of continuous improvement.

For the first time, these workers are linked together by a constant flow of suggestions, recommendations and ideas. These ideas concern nuts-and-bolts improvements on how to do their jobs better. And they are originating with and being implemented by workers on the line.

It began with the great American innovation of Walter Shewhart. His idea was simple: Put the means for managing quality and encouraging better and better performance in the hands of those who are actually doing the work. This bedrock business principle was

171

superbly refined by the Japanese and is now coming back and being discovered anew by more and more operations in the US.

The new management initiatives are sometimes classic continuous-improvement techniques, introduced directly by the great American pioneers in quality improvement who are still actively at work. More often, managers struggle to implement ideas they've read about or heard about in seminars. Sometimes companies such as Boardroom create their own successful systems, such as "I" Power.

Combining pragmatism with improvisation and eagerness to try something new, a whole new crop of department and plant managers, engineers and production managers and some courageous top managements are pushing away the barriers of traditional "scientific management." They are bringing in continuous-improvement techniques to assure the success of new operations and to revive the older ones.

For nearly two years, I crisscrossed the US talking to the managers and workers engaged in this Great Revival of American industry.

The following chapters represent three stories of how change is working...in a brand-new plant built on the eastern edge of the Rockies...in the giant processing complex of a great, well-established American company ...in one of the first big plants built after World War II in the Mississippi Delta, when firms from the North and the Midwest began to set down roots in what would eventually come to be known as the Sunbelt.

New York City   Marion Buhagiar
July, 1998

When a small group of us first came out here to Colorado in 1986 to plan this plant, we said: We have a fresh opportunity. Let's get it right. Let's see if we can build something that will make people feel good about the place they work in, be more productive and generate a quality product.

—Jack Carmichael,* Plant Manager, 1986–92
Anheuser-Busch's Fort Collins Brewery

40. Building In Improvement At Anheuser-Busch's Newest Brewery

1986. It had been a decade since Anheuser-Busch had built a new brewery in the US, a decade in which quality and tough competitive performance had come to matter as never before—in beer, too. The company's goal for the new brewery in Fort Collins, Colorado—its first in the Rocky Mountain area—was to establish continuous improvement in production operations from the beginning.

In essence, the company had already embraced the principles of continuous improvement.

Now Anheuser-Busch would apply these principles throughout the whole process of building and operating a massive, technologically complex and superbly modern brewery, building in continuous improvement from the ground up.

The evidence of success at Fort Collins is now on the

*Jack Carmichael is now plant manager at the Anheuser-Busch brewery in Williamsburg, Virginia.

173

record. Each year all 12 Anheuser-Busch breweries compete in the company's Reach for Excellence program by measuring themselves against *their own past-year performance* in 35 financial, quality and employee performance categories. In 1989, the first year Fort Collins became eligible to compete (it shipped its first beer in 1988), it won top rank—the coveted Golden Award. It won the Golden Award again in 1990, followed by the Silver Award in 1991.

The new plant's quality performance ranked high, too, with beer drinkers. Products produced at Fort Collins generated the second-fewest number of consumer complaints among the company's 12 breweries.

There are great lessons to be learned from Anheuser-Busch on how to make a new facility more and more productive by building in opportunities for ideas and suggestions to flow from the bottom up.

- Keep managers physically close to operations to facilitate communication with line workers and quick resolution of problems.
- Put new technology and new techniques in their places—*behind* encouraging employee efforts to come up with common-sense solutions to problems.
- Give employees the information they need to make productive suggestions for improving operations.
- Put a high priority on evaluating and rewarding middle managers according to their ability to encourage worker input.
- Reward every suggestion, no matter how small, that is implemented by the company. Small gifts, such as hats, shirts and recognition in the plant newsletter, work as well as monetary rewards.

KEEP MANAGERS PHYSICALLY CLOSE TO OPERATIONS

The plant manager of the Fort Collins brewery sits in a ground-floor office just inside the modest front lobby of the new complex built on the eastern edge of the Rocky Mountains. It's less than a minute's walk for him—through his secretary's area, down a short corridor and through a door on the right—to the plant floor and its shiny stainless-steel brew kettles, straining tanks, mash tanks, cooling towers, fermentation vats and filtering apparatus. If he opens the corridor door to the left, the manager steps into the packaging area, where bottles and cans swiftly flow along—filled, sealed, packed into cases and stacked on pallets for shipping.

As the first plant manager at Fort Collins, Jack Carmichael helped build just the kind of plant he wanted to run. From the ground up, it's been designed to ease the flow of information and suggestions from employees to solve problems and improve operations.

In traditional brewery operations, beer is processed in a separate complex.

Packaging has its own area, and so do maintenance and storerooms.

Engineers' offices are in a special section, and managers may well be in a completely different building.

People in administration at this new brewery, however, are *in the plant itself*. They can't look out of their office windows, notice that it's raining and decide that they don't have to walk over to the plant that day.

In the three-story building Anheuser-Busch built in Fort Collins, the most likely location for *executive* offices—traditionally—would be the third floor, with windows on all four sides and a spectacular panorama of the Rockies. Not here, though. The top floor of the plant is the company's cafeteria. And just as it is at all Anheuser-Busch breweries, there's no management dining room, no reserved tables.

All the Fort Collins managers work on the brewery plant's ground floor. Outside, they park their cars wherever they find a space. There's no reserved parking.

Managers and engineers work off a corridor that runs right down the middle of the plant. Engineers, maintenance managers and quality-assurance chemists bump into one another all the time—going to a meeting, to the rest rooms, to the cafeteria.

People who see one another all the time are forced to build a kind of camaraderie. But friendly feelings alone would never have been enough to make the plant effective.

Problems were to be expected from new, state-of-the-art equipment (notoriously vulnerable to "bugs" and shakedown delays) installed in the plant. An almost completely new work force—500 to 600 employees, the majority of whom were hired away from rural occupations or local firms, few with any experience in working with fluid processing or on packaging lines—also created the potential for plenty of problems.

Adding to the problem potential: During the plant's start-up year, the new managers and inexperienced work force had to master not only traditional brewing processes but complex new techniques. That year Anheuser-Busch pioneered three new products— Michelob Dry, cold-filtered (nonpasteurized) Busch Light and Bud Dry.

There were problems at Fort Collins, of course. But managers, engineers and brewmasters worked many of them out as quickly as they surfaced because they were in such close contact with plant operations, with one another—and with the employees learning the processes for the first time.

APPLY EMPLOYEE COMMON SENSE TO HELP SOLVE
NEW-TECHNOLOGY PROBLEMS

State-of-the-art equipment that promises to deliver high production- and labor-cost savings can have a hypnotic effect on managers striving to improve performance. They often hope that if they automate everything, they wouldn't need people and all their problems would go away.

Equally seductive for some managers: Seminars, books and programs that offer packaged (and often pat) solutions to what are often very specific problems in an organization.

Both technology and technique are important. But managers who successfully implement continuous-improvement systems generally conclude they are less important than organizing work to leave ample room for employees to use their own common sense to solve problems that surface in their work and come up with ways to improve the process itself.

The new manager's view: So-called technical wonders prove time and time again that if you don't apply common sense and emphasize the value of human beings involved in the process, you can wind up with the smartest—but the worst—operation in the world.

For example, problems kept popping up on the palletizer used to stack cases at the end of the packaging line for a forklift to pick up. When the palletizer jammed, the whole line shut down. And it kept jamming.

When efforts by plant engineers to debug operation of the equipment seemed to be going too slowly, Carmichael asked them to solicit ideas from the operators who worked on the line. The workers had plenty: Make this part and that part more substantial. Put Teflon on the metal table so cases shift around more easily. Each was a small contribution—a common-sense response to the operators' day-to-day experience of how the line functioned. Put together, though, they solved the palletizer jamming problem.

The lesson: Be alert to—and get rid of—barriers to communication that arise between operators and supervisors.

GIVE EMPLOYEES THE INFORMATION THEY NEED

If employees are to apply common sense effectively to improve the processes at which they work, they must have easy access to reliable information—both about the immediate production processes in which they are involved and about the way their specific job tasks fit into the company's overall business. Managers often fail by refusing to share information with employees for fear workers who know too much will use the information against them and against the operation. Managers like Carmichael say: "I know that the more employees know, the more they help. Sometimes they're so eager for more information so they can help that we can't get it to them fast enough."

Employees at the Fort Collins brewery are continually being educated, and that education ranges from the most fundamental level—how to use their equipment and monitor the plant's processes—to the broadest, company-wide perspective—where the company's strongest competition is now, how the plant's goals and performance fit into the company's overall strategy.

The responsibilities of production operators have been broadened.

- Workers don't just monitor a control panel or a piece of machinery. They take readings themselves that, in many of the nation's breweries, are taken only by supervisors.
- They are encouraged to contribute their experi-

ence and skills to the "professional-level" work of designing more effective equipment, processes and work flows. *Example:* The project to add a new can line to Fort Collins in 1989 was so big and important that engineers were brought in from corporate headquarters to work with the Fort Collins plant engineers. Despite this engineering heavy artillery, packaging-line workers at Fort Collins made a number of significant contributions to details of the line's ultimate design.

- They take far more responsibility for quality at the point of production. Operators are alert to pressure or temperature changes that might affect the brew's quality and are trained to take corrective action promptly on their own whenever possible.
- Line operators often call in mechanics themselves —rather than wait for a supervisor to make a decision and give an order—when they identify a piece of equipment that needs an adjustment or repair they cannot make themselves.

The goal is to push decision-making down to the lowest possible level, and to do it without a lot of buzzwords and faddish talk about new techniques and practices.

Because of the immediacy of face-to-face contact by operators, engineers and managers, and the sharing of essential information, Fort Collins operates without too much stair-step bureaucracy—moving problems up to the next level (and maybe the level above that, etc.) for a decision and back down again to implement. Many day-to-day problems are solved on the spot, quickly and without involving scores of people.

Of course, Anheuser-Busch also has a well-established formal system for keeping workers educated about how their own production-line responsibilities fit into the company's performance goals and need to meet competitive challengers.

The company-wide information program at Anheuser-Busch includes:

- A corporate meeting once a year at each brewery. Operations are shut down for a time on each shift while a senior manager from the St. Louis headquarters gives the shift's workers a personal report on company successes and competitive challenges. The briefing is followed by questions from the floor.

- Once-a-year plant-wide meetings at which the plant manager and resident brewmaster relate performance goals for the plant itself to company-wide objectives.

- Twice-a-year meetings in each brewery at which department heads (for brewing, engineering, packaging, quality assurance, warehousing, inventory control, business administration) exchange information on their operations and any issues that concern them.

This was not enough for the plant manager and the resident brewmaster at Fort Collins, however.

In 1988, they adopted one idea pioneered at another Anheuser-Busch brewery and began to sit down three or four times a month with a cross section of 15 or so operators and technicians from the plant and its support operations.

No agenda is set for the meetings. The plant manager and the brewmaster ask open-ended questions: "What's on your minds? What questions do you have about what's been going on? What ideas do you have for doing things better around here?"

In many companies, managers have little tolerance for such meetings. They object to spending an hour or so at an agenda-less meeting as "a waste of time." Or, more contemptuously, they denounce these frequent contacts with production-level workers as "baby-sitting."

Carmichael, though, says he has never had such a meeting without a gain: "I always find something we have to look into."

In fact, these grassroots meetings are producing so many ideas and are so effective in alerting top plant executives to areas that need attention that the company's top management at St. Louis suggested that every brewery management team add similar meetings to its information program.

EVALUATE AND REWARD MIDDLE MANAGERS ACCORDING TO THEIR ABILITY TO ENCOURAGE WORKER INPUT

Once Carmichael initiated the weekly, nonagenda meetings, he found out—to his surprise—that the flow of communication between operators and top management seemed to be easier and more complete than it was between those employees and middle managers.

"The employees seemed to understand what I wanted and what the brewmaster wanted," Carmichael explains. "But they weren't really sure what the people in the middle ranks wanted or expected of them. They seemed to think of middle management as a kind of mystery area."

Carmichael was surprised because he had already anticipated such a problem—and thought he was well prepared for it. Management had carefully screened prospective managers for the new plant to select those who seemed most responsive to encouraging the flow of ideas from below. One key part of the screening: How the prospect seemed to take to the no-nonsense statement of principles drafted to guide the design of the plant and subsequent brewery operations.

The statement is full of such phrases as "encourage involvement," "acknowledge individual and group achievements in a timely manner" and "provide for individual growth and development." In staffing the plant, management passed over some manager-candidates with excellent technical credentials and experience because they seemed inflexible and too devoted to more traditional (and authoritarian) industrial-management practices.

But clearly, such screening wasn't enough. Well-meaning intentions and sensitivity to the value of employee ideas don't by themselves prime the pump. The temptation to let all decisions and ideas originate at the top and flow down is so great that even the well-screened managers at Fort Collins had to be strongly encouraged to produce suggestions and ideas from operators and technicians.

There are several strategies in place now to encourage the flow of communication.

- A middle manager is invited, along with operators and technicians, to sit in on each of the weekly grassroots meetings with the plant manager and the brewmaster to hear (and respond to, if he/she chooses) what the people on the line say and ask.
- When new equipment is being designed or installed for the plant, managers are asked: "Did you ask the operators what they think?" *The risk this avoids:* Later on, when there's a problem, some manager or engineer will ask the operators: "Why can't you guys get this line to work properly?" And the operators will say: "We didn't design it. You did."

Like many able managers, Carmichael "manages by walking around" the plant—but with a significant difference added by systems to encourage problem-solving and ideas from the bottom up. Once, as a young and conscientious plant manager, he thought knowing everything was the only way to be sure that the plant ran well. Now, he says, he needs to uncover and grapple with only the significant things.

He can trust others to handle many things that used to be only management's job. Problems are solved. Good decisions are made. And nobody at the top has to take any particular notice of it.

REWARDING EMPLOYEE SUGGESTIONS—FORMALLY AND INFORMALLY

As company suggestion systems go, the company-wide one at Anheuser-Busch, formalized in 1982, is one of the most enlightened and effective.

It has faced up to the most common barriers to suggestion systems in American companies—slow response and failure to implement. An Anheuser-Busch employee who makes a suggestion can expect to get a reply within 30 days. One of the measures of management performance at each of the company's dozen breweries is the average time it takes to respond to employee suggestions.

Anheuser-Busch estimates that it realizes about $7.6 million in net annual savings from its suggestion program. But money isn't all. The program encourages communication links among all levels and rewards employees and managers for developing and demonstrating initiative and ingenuity.

Why many company suggestion systems are so barren: They too often get hung up on the negatives—why an idea *won't* work.

The reason is that negatives are often where management typically focuses its attention—a negative variance in the budget, a product coming off the line out of spec. But smooth production, a really great run—managers rarely think that is worth a remark, though they are very likely to be right in there to criticize that same high-performing crew if there's a problem.

At Fort Collins, employee contributions to improvement are not limited to plant operations. Since many of the plant's workers are also consumers of beer, they often volunteer their observations on how Anheuser-Busch (and competitor) products are displayed in local stores, stocked at bars and restaurants. They quickly spot new products or tactics competitors are using. They report on how their friends and other customers appear to be responding to the new products or marketing. This information is quickly sent to marketing and sales departments for evaluation and response.

Fort Collins managers often don't wait for the formal or gift-certificate rewards to be generated by the corporate suggestion program. Every implemented suggestion, no matter how small, is rewarded.

The goal: Recognize any achievement in the brewery that is significant. Nothing splashy. A new baseball cap to wear in the brewery. Free lunch. Free dessert. It depends on what the contribution is at the time. The steady stream of small, timely gifts encourages wider participation by employees.

NINE LESSONS FOR STEADY IMPROVEMENT FROM ANHEUSER-BUSCH

1. Keep managers physically as close to the center of operations as possible. Encourage informal encounters among managers and between managers and employees who process the work. But don't interpret "management by walking around" to mean that the manager has to know everything that is going on at the plant. The more successful the continuous-improvement system you put in place, the fewer the decisions that must be made at the top. The walking around is to encourage communication and applaud performance—not to inspect and correct.

2. Don't give technique, technology or procedures priority over good communication that encourages employees to use their own common sense. Cut-and-dried systems in which an employee either does a job right or wrong leave no room for gray areas—which is just where common sense works best. Being able to cope with all the things in between is what makes the difference between an effective and a mediocre operation and between a valuable and good employee and somebody who is just there—a body, a number.

3. Share information with employees. The more they know about the machines they work with, how the process fits into the overall operation and what the quality standards are, the more they can contribute.

4. Good intentions by managers (or saying the right thing) are never enough to unlock the flow of good ideas from below. Top managers must be vigilant in making sure that middle managers, technicians and professionals enlist ideas in day-to-day operations. Open communication and encouragement of common-sense solutions can be just as important as written-down procedures.

5. Make effectiveness at continuous improvement a key measure of each manager's performance. Rank plants, divisions or departments by how much they improve over their own past performance in certain critical areas. Make quick response to employee suggestions one of the critical areas that is measured.

6. When designing, buying or installing new equipment and processes, encourage managers and engineers to actively enlist suggestions and ideas from employees who will be using the equipment or process.

7. Set up nonagenda, one-hour meetings on a frequent schedule (once a week is good) between senior managers and employees processing the work in various

parts of the organization. Have one member of middle management sit in on each meeting, too.

8. Carefully recruit and promote middle managers who are flexible and ready to encourage employee suggestions.

9. If the company produces products or services that are widely available to consumers, don't limit employees to suggestions for improving work processes. Give them responsibility for improving the performance of the company in the marketplace, too. Encourage them to compare company products and services with those of competitors and to report lack of product, messy displays or new introductions and promotions by competitors. Make sure employee observations are given serious consideration by sales or marketing, and report back to employees if any action is taken in response to the information they gather.

Continuous improvement is not just another thing that we manage here—something off to the side that management is doing. This process structure we now have in place for improvement is the way we manage our business. No matter what we do, it has to fit into continuous improvement.
　　　　　　　　—Mike Easley, Manufacturing Services Manager,
　　　　　　　　Baxter Healthcare, Cleveland, Mississippi, Plant

41. Taking Control Of Their Own Destiny At Baxter Healthcare

Baxter Healthcare Corporation's plant in the heart of the Mississippi Delta country was an anxious place in late 1985. Built in 1949 on Highway 61, which runs flat and straight for hundreds of miles south of Memphis, Tennessee, through rice, soy bean and cotton farmland and small Delta towns, the Baxter plant has been the biggest employer in Cleveland, Mississippi, ever since. But employment at the plant peaked in the early 1970s, at about 2,300 jobs. By 1985, only 750 people worked there.

Even the future of those jobs was in doubt. Baxter Travenol Laboratories, Inc. had recently merged with the other big hospital-supply company, American Hospital Supply Corporation. Faced with excess manufacturing capacity, management set to work consolidating operations to make them more efficient.

A number of the product lines at the Cleveland plant could be headed out the door in 1986, was the worry of

187

plant managers.

They had to take control of their destiny.

That's what the employees at the Cleveland plant did—successfully—by equipping every operator and supervisor with the skills and knowledge they needed to constantly improve quality, efficiency and productivity.

They turned the whole factory around. By January 1992, employment at the plant was up almost 90 percent, to about 1,400 workers. A key quality measure—defects per million products produced—went down 60 percent from 1988 to 1991. Manufacturing time required to get out key product lines was also down 60 percent. Inventory turns on one product line went up 199 percent, on another 170 percent and on another 94 percent. None improved less than 20 percent.

Costs came down steadily.

The improvements at Cleveland have been rewarded. Instead of operations moving out of the plant, Baxter's top management decided to move some *in*—new injection molding and extrusion operations from other Baxter facilities, for instance. The Cleveland plant has been expanding, while elsewhere Baxter trimmed its sails.

Nowadays, it probably has the most diverse group of manufacturing operations of any Baxter facility. It makes more than 400 different product codes for hospitals, manufacturing for nine different Baxter divisions. The quality of the output from Cleveland is so high and its processes so effective that it manages to be competitive even in assembling complex, custom-designed sets used for specialized hospital treatments—a line of business where mom-and-pop shops around the country have carved out tiny market niches.

Results at the Baxter Cleveland plant owe everything to the principles of continuous improvement.

- All employees undergo fundamental training in the modern techniques of statistical control, problem-solving and teamwork. More intense training is given on an application by application basis.

- Managers make sincere efforts to find out from the employees what they need, what is going well—and what is not.
- Employees on the product lines are all encouraged to use their greater knowledge and understanding of the processes on which they work to make suggestions on how to do things better.
- The work force as a whole has a clear focus on what the priorities for improvement are—and when they change.

The first step in taking destiny into their own hands at Baxter was an accelerated training program. The aim was to introduce everyone—managers, supervisors, operators—to quality-management techniques that they could use to monitor their own output. Employees quickly learned how—and why—to keep quality performance charts and use them to monitor their own output.

Line operators and supervisors were unbound from narrow departmental and functional responsibilities and encouraged to work on product-line teams that focused on ways to improve work flows, solve bottlenecks, reduce defects.

Vital lessons in taking control learned at Baxter Cleveland:

- Intense employee training is essential. First, it increases knowledge. Just as important: It helps overcome cynicism and suspicions about management's commitment to acting on employees' ideas for continuous improvement of the company's operations.
- Survey employees regularly for their frank feed-

back on what's working, what they feel is lacking.

- Provide continual support for employees by educating them about tools and techniques that can be useful to them in day-to-day work. Continuous improvement does not work on hype...it works on knowledge and commitment.
- Once a continuous-improvement process is working reasonably well within the plant (or department or company), move it outside—to customers, to suppliers. And make use of benchmarking to compare the effectiveness of your operations with that of the acknowledged best in the business. Don't move too quickly on this. First make sure you have good data and facts on your *own* operations. Then, and only then, can you get the best out of benchmarking with high-performing operations elsewhere in the company or at other companies.
- Devise simple systems to monitor team activities and meetings to make sure there is full participation, to keep efforts on track and to identify progress.
- Keep an eye on costs—and cost reduction—especially after the initial period of heavy training to introduce quality-management techniques and team work. Otherwise senior management may lose patience with the effort. Some results will begin to show *immediately*.

HOW—AND WHY—BAXTER'S MANAGERS JUMP-STARTED TRAINING

Meeting quality standards is an old, familiar business at Baxter, because plants like that at Cleveland run under US Food and Drug Administration guidelines. These establish documentation rules to assure timely release of quality products used for blood transfusions, infusions, dialysis and other medical procedures.

Until 1986, however, there was no formal structure at the Cleveland plant designed to generate continuous improvements in quality throughout the operation. The managers of the Cleveland plant decided that an aggressive and successful effort to improve quality would be the best way to assure the survival of their operation, once Baxter's top management began making tough decisions about shifting and consolidating operations.

The effort started at the grassroots—education of the existing work force at Cleveland. That was the basis of turning the plant around, in the opinion of Mike Easley, manufacturing services manager at the Baxter plant.

Late in 1985, outside consultants began to train Cleveland managers to begin the quality-management process. No time to lose. But the "quality gurus" projected that the training cycle would take 12 to 18 months. That was too long for managers, who felt they were in a race against time to show what the plant could do. So the managers quickly expanded training downward to the first-line supervisor level. By January 1986, operators from the plant floor, too, were being trained.

In *eight* months, every employee at Cleveland had successfully completed the training. There was no cut in content. What made this accomplishment even more remarkable was that a number of the operators who completed the training and now make major contributions to improving work processes were deficient in basic reading skills when training started.

Management used several methods to accelerate the progress of the training...

- Relying on their close understanding of the Cleveland plant's processes, managers and supervisors adapted training materials supplied by outside consultants—adding and deleting elements to customize the program.

- Scheduling the 24-hour operation of the plant to accommodate training became a priority. Lines were shut down entirely for a time so that groups of employees could "go to school." Managers also arranged schedules to make sure that employees from different operations and managers with different functional responsibilities were often learning together at the same training sessions.

- Setting a firm rule that everybody had to go through every scheduled training class—no exceptions and very few make-up sessions.

It was tough to hold the line, because initially some supervisors tried very hard to convince senior plant management that they had to stay out there in the trenches rather than go to a training session. The message back to them from management: "You're no different from anyone else. You have to make every session or you won't graduate." *Result:* Peers competed to be the first to complete the training process.

Typical training sessions consisted of about 15 minutes of review of materials by an instructor, followed by about 45 minutes of applying the techniques described in the materials directly to real work. Attendance and completed homework assignments became the basis of awards that management gave to best-performing teams.

GETTING EVERYONE TO "BUY IN"

The intensity of that eight-month training period overcame a great deal of the typical first line of resistance to most new management programs—"This is just another fad that will be gone by next year."

Added to that inevitable cynicism, this time, was fear. At first people were really frightened by the notion of achieving zero defects. They felt it meant they could never make a mistake.

How managers handled the fears: They took time to explain carefully that zero defects is a goal you want to strive for by working on continuous improvements. It's a philosophy that you will never be satisfied with less than perfection and must keep moving toward that point. You're never satisfied with the status quo.

The advantages of a continuous-improvement process are never so obvious to employees that they simply buy in without resistance once management initiates the idea.

The typical process goes something like this. An eager-for-change group—usually 15 to 30 percent of the work-force—signs on first, often giving false hope to managers that everyone else will soon be in step, too. Not so. Most of the time, after this first spurt of enthusiasm, the process is challenged. Problems surface. Teams fail. *Worst of all:* In many companies, management commitment begins to fade at this point. Managers neglect supporting teams with feedback and resources.

The only way to move beyond this point is for managers to keep the program going until some of the older, more experienced employees are won over. They are often the ones who initially withhold wholehearted support, because they have seen management enthusiasm for new programs wax and wane over the years. "Those workers put a little more of a fire test to you," says Easley. But that's not all bad.

Eventually, these experienced workers cooperate because they begin to recognize values in continuous improvement that didn't exist in previous efforts to upgrade performance. Their acceptance of the program carries great weight with others. The momentum of the whole process begins to climb up more steeply.

Baxter was fortunate in that the top management recognized the value of the initiatives taken at the Cleveland plant quite quickly. As a result, the plant was asked to share what it learned with other operations in the company. In a sense it became a benchmark for them. That improved the plant's image throughout the company... that plus the results that the process generated.

HOW BAXTER GOT FEEDBACK—WHY BAXTER NEEDED FEEDBACK

Even though top management at Baxter began to encourage the changes that were taking place at the Cleveland plant, the plant's managers knew that potential dangers still existed. They had to keep momentum building among the employees, involve more and more of them in initiating improvements. Encouraging honest feedback from the plant's employees about their experiences with the new system turned out to be an excellent lever for generating wider support and participation.

The primary tool was a regular series of surveys in which employees could raise questions, identify their concerns, make clear what they felt worked best and challenge the continuous-improvement process as it evolved.

The first surveys—taken during the initial training period—gave everyone an opportunity to try out their newly learned expertise. The simple, two-part survey first described an actual quality problem that developed at the plant, then the action a supervisor had taken to solve the problem.

Each employee was asked to critique the solution and answer the questions: Was this the right way to solve the problem? Is there a better way?

These initial surveys guided management in strengthening the training program. Replies brought out some fundamental questions about the sincerity of management's effort. For instance, employees quickly raised a key question: Which comes first, quality or cost reduction?

Consistent tracking by surveys kept management tuned in to how people actually felt about the process. How management was dealing with their concerns. And whether or not management answered their questions.

To put it most simply, the people in the plant gave managers their priorities instead of the other way around.

It took three years of patient work and attention to survey replies to reach the point at Baxter's Cleveland plant where only a few diehards still resisted active participation in the continuous-improvement process.

"The desire to participate more and more in the process jumps right out at you," Easley explains. "Virtually all plant employees are now anxious to find a way to fit in. They're convinced that management is really committed to the change. And they can see clearly that the change is good for the operation of the plant, good for their jobs, good for their future."

TURNING TRAINING INTO ACTIONS

No continuous-improvement process can survive just on the commitment of employees for higher quality production. As many companies have found to their disappointment, the general exhilaration at the initial stage can fizzle quickly. Managers must support employees with tools, resources and follow-up training. At every level, employees have to grasp the techniques they need to carry out work at this new and higher level of responsibility.

The improvement in output and efficiency is directly related to improving the skills of the production employees and their ability to work in teams. They must have an opportunity to learn about and understand the whole process, not just their own jobs within that process.

Managers must keep in touch with teams in order to understand when workers need training in new techniques to solve problems or when they need more up-to-date tools and equipment. "Teams," says Easley, "are where the rubber meets the road."

At the Cleveland plant, operators are now taught basic skills in machine maintenance so that they can handle routine adjustments and repairs themselves rather than shut down the machine (and perhaps the line) to wait for mechanics. Maintenance operators are adept at analyzing the data output from vibration monitors to predict information to identify early warning signals that a piece of equipment is likely to fail. They can extend the life of machines by shutting them down so that the problem can be fixed *before* there is a mechanical failure.

One team that operates a high-speed line to label and pack bottles of fluid struggled for months to debug a custom-designed machine built by an outside contractor. The machine went down again and again. Finally, the team concluded that it would be better for them to redesign and rebuild an altogether new unit on their own. They did, and it ran for six months with no downtime.

Rather than wait for orders, teams gather facts, analyze data, predict where problems are likely to show up—and often prevent them. They are eager to use new measuring tools and equipment, such as high-speed video cameras that enable them to analyze the synchronization of a process on a high-speed machine frame by frame to identify problems such as timing that they cannot see with their own eyes.

FUNCTIONS AND DYSFUNCTIONS

Within a year after the continuous-improvement reforms were put in place at the Cleveland plant, it became clear that even though the teams were growing more powerful in skills, understanding and initiative, something was holding them back. The barrier was the management organization of the plant itself.

The organization chart for the Cleveland plant looked no different from that of most manufacturing operations in the US. Baxter had separate departments for filling, packing, sterilization, etc., and each was headed by a superintendent.

Within each department, individual employees and newly founded teams achieved higher performance levels—such as increasing the number of solution bottles filled without defects. Often, though, there was little overall value to the plant in those achievements. Filled bottles, for instance, might just stand around because there weren't enough sterilization trucks to move output along at the increased rate.

Neither operators, teams nor department superintendents had a good enough overall perspective of the process flow for the products they produced. This nearsightedness made it difficult to train workers and managers to use inventory-saving (and cost-reducing) techniques, such as just-in-time production.

The solution: Superintendents were given total product-line responsibilities. Support functions such as industrial engineering were assigned responsibility by product lines. Most teams also took on product-line rather than department responsibility. (A few teams—for instance, materials logistics and supplier relations—continued to function as facilitators with a plant-wide focus.)

Starting cautiously, the managers at Cleveland made up their first product-line teams almost solely with administrative and salaried employees. As confidence grew and management saw that product-line team efforts could be controlled and directed, more and more hourly employees were added to the teams. By 1991, teams began to set up subteams, primarily made up of hourly employees, to work on specific projects. For the most part, these subteams carry out their work successfully with no supervisory members.

STEERING CHANGE IN THE RIGHT DIRECTION

Enthusiasm, training, the right tools and equipment, recognition, support and continuing encouragement by management and product-line responsibility generates commitment to higher quality performance virtually everywhere it's tried. *But even that's not enough.*

There were lots of activities going on at the Cleveland plant—lots of teams and committees. But managers could see that it wasn't as smooth as it should be.

Focusing that effort in a direction likely to yield the most value became the next management task.

The first step toward focusing effort had been reorganizing plant management and teams along product lines. That was now backed up by building a new information and communication structure.

- Managers make frequent reviews of what teams are doing—to avoid overlapping projects and to assure that the focus of team efforts matches management priorities.
- Managers make sure teams are fine-tuned and balanced—to make sure that they have people with the right skills and the resources they need to pursue their goals. *Guideline:* Align teams so that they don't duplicate effort. But don't limit the work of the teams when they are really on focus.
- Measure and monitor the improvement trend.

The minutes of weekly team meetings turned out to be a key tool in keeping team efforts on track. At first these minutes followed the typical stale, rambling narrative form of most organization minutes. Managers who reviewed and discussed the minutes at their own weekly meetings frankly admitted that they had a hard time keeping track of progress or getting a clear signal when a team was stalled and needed help.

The solution: A clear, standard form that all team minutes now follow, making it easy for managers to scan the information.

Control is *not* the prime reason to standardize the ways teams report. The goal is focus and simplicity.

Managers *have* to pay attention to what teams are doing or the teams die, in Easley's experience. The Cleveland way to make them pay attention is to make it easy to review and discuss team activities at a weekly steering committee meeting.

In addition to the review of team minutes, each week, in rotation, one of the teams makes a personal report to the steering committee on actions, progress and problems so that the managers on the steering committee can meet and talk directly to team members.

Baxter's Cleveland plant is now well past the stage when the continuous-improvement teams might be considered just another management fad.

Progress and success are obvious. The whole process is now ingrained. The likelihood of a particular team failing is less and less. In fact, says Easley, they can't work without teams anymore.

MEASURING PROGRESS

In every part of the Cleveland plant, improvement in effectiveness is reflected in progress charts that clearly display an area's achievement toward goals on costs, inventory, quality and process capability (how quickly and efficiently a product moves through the plant).

Making sure such progress is measured and made public is a key management responsibility. Employees believe improvement is important when management takes the time to train them in how to measure their own progress and reinforces the need for such measurement.

The first step in measuring progress is to agree on a balanced set of indicators (called a *scorecard*) for product lines, to be measured for improvement each quarter. At Cleveland, these indicators are grouped under categories: Process Flow, Inventory, Quality, Costs.

Next, work out a point system so that an overall trend line can be plotted as well as performance in each category. Chart that data each quarter. Make sure every employee clearly understands what factors go into calculating the points—so they know what they have to do to improve performance.

Don't get bogged down by attempting to make the point system accurate down to the decimal point. Make it accurate enough to show *relative* progress.

Share the information on the scorecards about overall as well as area performance widely throughout the workplace. Use the results to guide and monitor team priorities and progress.

Finally, recognize achievement. For example, when a department meets its suggestion-system goals at the Cleveland plant, the whole department is served a steak dinner at the plant cafeteria—tablecloths, good table service—right in the midst of all the other employees eating at that time. And the Cleveland team that demonstrates the best overall performance for the year receives an award that has come to be regarded by all plant employees as extremely prestigious: Team of the Year.

LINKING CUSTOMERS AND SUPPLIERS INTO BAXTER'S IMPROVEMENT EFFORT

Moving the lessons of continuous improvement and teamwork beyond the walls of the Cleveland plant has required patient work. Rewarding work. The exchange of information with other companies, suppliers and customers levers up the quality of change at the plant itself.

The first step outside was the easiest: Transferring knowledge about what was working well at Cleveland to other Baxter units. Within a year of the program's start-up there were enough visible results—less scrap, lower defect rate, better use of resources—for managers in other Baxter plants to want to visit and see what was happening.

Benchmarking came later—comparing technical processes such as injection molding and sterilization as done at the Cleveland plant with the practices at other high-performing facilities. It wasn't something they could rush into.

Benchmarking is most useful only after you know a lot about your own operations. If your own process isn't clearly organized and you don't have the details and the right data about your own operation, you cannot make useful comparisons.

Most recently, the teams at the Cleveland plant have been extending their reach outward to Baxter customers in their search for improvements. The plant maintains a joint working team with a local hospital. Nurses who use Baxter products in hospitals come to the plant to show employees exactly how the products are used on patients. Plant employees and supervisors tour hospitals to see how the products they make are handled by end users.

These connections with end users are now having an impact on decisions made at the plant itself. A team of managers and operators at the plant was about to move ahead on changes in the blood-plasma product line, for instance. As part of the process of change, some team members visited a blood-plasma center. After taking into account how the products they made were actually used, the team concluded that the changes under consideration would lead to less satisfactory product performance in the hands of customers. So the proposed changes were abandoned.

TYING A FORMAL SUGGESTION PROGRAM INTO CONTINUOUS IMPROVEMENT

On the brightly lit wall just outside the Cleveland plant cafeteria is the plant's Wall of Fame—a display of photograph portraits of numerous plant employees who have won awards for the quality and frequency of their suggestions for improving plant operations.

The suggestion system at Cleveland now, put into place in 1986, is not typical. Unlike the old personnel suggestion system it replaced, which was a if-you-have-a-problem-let-us-know sort of thing, the current system is designed to be part of the overall continuous-improvement process.

How the suggestion system works:
- Every idea is acknowledged within 24 hours. Within five days, the person who made a suggestion gets a report on what action is being taken on it.
- Ideas don't get lost. All of them are immediately entered into a computerized data bank, which at any time can print out the status of each idea submitted.
- The implementation rate on suggestions is above 90 percent.
- Ideas are each evaluated for their *quality*. The top managers of the plant meet regularly to grade

ideas—with points—against weighted criteria, including what the savings are, what it costs to implement the idea, the impact on product quality, regulatory issues affected. Intangible considerations earn points, too—for instance, does the suggestion eliminate some annoying hassle? (The criteria for rewarding points have been made clear to employees. And the first pass at grading suggestions is now done at the team level.)

- The person who submits the idea evaluated as Best of the Month has his/her photograph taken and displayed prominently—and also gets to use the plant or quality manager's parking spot for a week.

- Frequency of participation in the suggestion program is also rewarded with points. Accumulated points can be redeemed in "purchases" from a gift catalog.

- High-point individual ideas can achieve bronze, silver or gold recognition.

Managers at the Cleveland plant do not measure the success of the suggestion system by cost savings. That is just one of the program's goals. The improvement goals for the suggestion program are an improved suggestion system. The progress thus far:

- Number of ideas submitted—up from 197 in 1987 to 1,707 in 1991.

- Percent of employees who make suggestions—up from 25 percent in 1990 to 56 percent in 1991.

Important, too, is the source of the suggestions. Initially most suggestions came from supervisors and professionals working in support functions. In recent years the balance has shifted sharply. Now *most* of the ideas originate with the people who work right on the plant floor.

REDUCING COSTS MATTERS, TOO

Costs at the Cleveland plant have come down steadily as quality and performance have gone steadily upward. This is in spite of the fact that cost reduction—often the number-one goal when plants are traditionally managed—is now only one of six goal categories for improvement at Cleveland.

When cost-cutting is the number one goal, the management priorities are familiar: Produce as much product as you can to absorb overhead expense and show low unit cost. Results are usually familiar, too: A hidden cost burden in excess inventories and obsolescence.

At Cleveland, work is now scheduled according to a policy that states: "We will reach agreement with our corporate interfaces and customers to determine production schedules that match demand and meet customer-service requirements at the best possible costs. Our production schedules will meet requirements on quantity, quality and time.

Nevertheless, costs did indeed go down right from the start of the continuous-improvement program, even though employees were going through extensive training and the team operations suffered growing pains. After the first couple of years, improvement shot up, and the reward has meant more and more to the bottom line.

The cruel fact is that unless they have evidence that costs have been brought under control, most senior managers quickly lose enthusiasm for the other achievements of continuous-improvement efforts.

TEN LESSONS FROM BAXTER'S EXPERIENCE WITH CONTINUOUS IMPROVEMENT

1. Integrate the improvement process into the overall management of an operation. Encouraging employees to contribute their ideas on doing things better is not just another "program." Every meeting, appraisal, review of operations, decision to change a product line or add new equipment must incorporate the practice of encouraging input from the people who will be involved in the specific process.

2. Low or mediocre literacy and math skills in the work force are not insurmountable barriers to putting in new techniques such as statistical process management. Take the literacy factor into account and put the emphasis on patience and thoroughness in training.

3. From the onset, insist that supervisors and managers attend all training sessions. (They are more likely to want to "skip" than lower-level employees.) Limit the number of make-up sessions to keep training on course. Make it a hard-and-fast rule that all employees complete all training. Reward completion by individuals and by departments.

4. Survey, survey, survey. Survey employees first about their expectations for the program. Then survey during training to assess their level of development and identify gaps. Encourage them to ask questions—and answer those questions promptly. As the effort matures, survey to find out what employees would do to improve the continuous-improvement system itself.

5. Combine any continuous-improvement effort with an organizational review—to eliminate functional divisions and barriers as much as possible. Organize as much as possible by product line rather than according to stages of production or function.

6. Regularly set priorities for improvement efforts. Encourage all suggestions for improvement, but make clear what management's priorities are for that period—and why.

7. Review the flow of suggestions and the activities of problem-solving teams at least once a month (or even more frequently) to make sure the focus matches management priorities. Simplify and standardize the reporting system so management can quickly review what's happening.

8. Find ways to measure improvement. Make the trend public. Evaluate employee improvement ideas for quality. Make the quality criteria clear. Relate the flow of ideas to priorities. Ask for suggestions on improving the criteria. Reward individuals and teams not only for quantity of suggestions but also for quality.

9. Once continuous improvement is running fairly smoothly within the operation, start moving out to suppliers and customers for their input. Share your success stories with them and encourage them to make similar efforts if they are not already doing it.

10. Never lose sight of costs. In its early stages—when training may be necessary—cost improvements may not be significant. But eventually the operation must show cost and productivity improvements to maintain management support.

To take risks, people have to trust. Before they trust, they have to be committed. Before they commit themselves, they have to come to an agreement on who is doing what. Management has to build the trust before it can get employees to make improvements consistently.
—Edward A. Tucker, Technical Advisor, Manufacturing
Excellence, Eastman Kodak Co., Windsor, Colorado

42. Overhauling
The Traditional
At Kodak

In the early 1980s, Eastman Kodak faced the same challenge of emerging foreign competition that would prove so costly to the then-dominant US auto and steel industries. Long the world's leading supplier of photographic goods, it relied on price to drive profitability.

But with the emergence of Fuji as a powerful price competitor, the world changed for Kodak. Profitability became a matter of controlling cost while at the same time improving quality.

Unlike many other US firms in a similar position, Kodak was able to respond successfully to the challenge and has retained its position as the world industry leader.

Some of the keys to this success can be seen in the operation of the company's Windsor, Colorado, plant, which produces the lion's share of the world's X-ray film and color paper for color prints. There, a production plant formerly run with highly structured, top-down management has been transformed into one driven by high-spirited employee initiative.

Kodak learned some vital lessons at Windsor, and they were lessons perfectly in tune with the principles of encouraging employee suggestions for continuous improvement.

- Move cautiously when changing from a very structured system of management to one that relies on employee initiative. Trust between employees and management is essential to overcome inevitable problems that result from change. Sudden change makes employees feel at jeopardy and undermines that trust.

- Involve employees in making decisions on purchasing new equipment the workers will have to operate, and in keeping equipment running smoothly. Being in on selecting new equipment and processes from the beginning increases their commitment to solving the problems that inevitably develop.

- Review the company's traditional suggestion and bonus systems to determine whether they support a new continuous-improvement program.

- Make "contribution to continuous improvement" and "ability to work in a team" key performance factors evaluated in employees' annual appraisals.

BUILDING TRUST COMES FIRST

Like many other American companies in the early 1980s, managers at Kodak Windsor joined the revival of interest in statistical quality controls. They also dabbled with Japanese-style "quality circles." The true believers in management taught the basic tools to anybody in the plant who would sit still and listen.

But the quality circles didn't survive. Inexperience and

lack of trust were two key reasons. Ironically, one of the problems was that managers didn't trust themselves to direct employees in the new relationship. They couldn't, at first, treat employees as equals in the problem-solving process. Afraid of overdirecting and of influencing quality circles with their own ideas, the managers went too far in the other direction. By their own admission, they "naively" thought the circles could work by themselves.

The managers didn't trust themselves, nor did they entirely trust employees. They tended to restrict the use of quality circles to narrow areas. As a result, the quality circles seemed to be working on projects that held only limited promise. They seemed to be making little headway toward significant improvement in the overall way in which work was done at Windsor.

The first impatient reaction of Kodak managers was that the employees were focusing only on things that had personal significance to them, whether or not it was important to improving operations at the plant. That reaction, too, may have been the product of management illusions.

Later, as they reviewed what went wrong, managers found out that the things quality circles elected to work on often had little significance, too, for the employees involved. They were going through the motions because managers appeared to want them to use the technique.

Inexperience, combined with eagerness to adopt ideas that would transform the Kodak operation, led managers to make other mistakes.

They put people together and called it a team even though the team members had no real work interrelationships, nothing in common and no common stake in what they were working on.

They didn't know what to reward. At the beginning they thought asking a team of employees to make a presentation to management on how they had solved a problem would be a big thing for them. But putting on presentations for senior managers was the last thing in the world most employees were interested in doing. Some of them felt as if they were back at school again with show-and-tell. The opportunity to make good presentations, it turned out, really was significant chiefly for the managers themselves.

Not all the setbacks on the road to continuous improvement were due to lack of understanding and experience. The first efforts toward a continuous-improvement system coincided with the first job layoffs at Kodak in the memory of most employees.

The layoffs came as a tremendous blow. This was a company, after all, in which job security had been largely taken for granted. Lost with the jobs was employee trust, just at a time when Kodak was asking workers to commit themselves more to improving the company's performance.

At Kodak, inexperience with the techniques of layoffs and firings made the first cut particularly rough. Employees at all levels, including managers, were given scant notice. Keeping the prospect of job cuts secret until the last minute was part of the same paternalistic culture at Kodak that "protected" jobs in the first place. Now managers thought they were "protecting" employees' feelings.

But as the managers at Windsor continued to pursue efforts to encourage employee initiative in solving problems, they recognized a growing need to put more and more effort into developing trust. They had come to realize its power.

In a more recent layoff at Windsor, for example, employees were given six months' notice. By now, say the managers, everyone who works at Windsor understands how their lives are impacted by how well the company does. Kodak is in a new global ball game, a highly competitive ball game. If it has to downsize five percent or ten percent, managers start by working together with employees to build a plan that serves, as fairly as possible, the needs of everyone affected but also accomplishes the goals that need to be met.

BUILDING COMMITMENT

Improvisation and pragmatism have become hallmarks of a wide array of continuous-improvement programs springing up at Windsor. False starts don't discourage people. When a small group of workers become motivated to try something, managers are disposed to let them do it—after considering the safety and quality issues.

Old work rules, for instance, are set aside as better ways of doing things are found. One senior manager still remembers vividly how, years ago, a plant superintendent chewed out a foreman whom he found running a forklift truck. The management message was: "We don't pay you to handle a truck. Never let me find you on one again!"

The foreman, though, had climbed on the truck to unload a machine in order to keep it operating. The man who usually ran the fork lift had been called away to help on an emergency in another part of the plant.

That foreman did the right thing in taking over that truck, the senior manager says now, given the wisdom of hindsight. The foreman had gotten nailed for doing something extra that wasn't in his job description. And you can bet he never did that again.

Mind you—there's no union at Kodak Windsor. No union work rules. Like a lot of companies, managers themselves developed a lot of union-type work rules that led to inefficient ways of running things. Now those managers are busy breaking down barriers they themselves had set up.

One of the most successful programs at Windsor is the chipping away at traditional boundaries between production operators who run machines and the maintenance crews who adjust and repair the units. The goal is to encourage employees who operate machines to take greater responsibility for keeping them running well, broadening rather than narrowing their responsibilities.

More flexibility between production and maintenance workers is the heart of a technique called Total Productive Maintenance, originally developed in Japanese factories. Windsor "imported" this idea but, unlike the other import—quality circles—this one took hold.

Managers at Kodak Windsor found out about the technique by talking with managers at Kodak's chemical plant in Tennessee, who had pioneered the idea within the company and, indeed, within the US. A couple of Windsor managers spent two days at the Tennessee plant and wrote up what they saw. Soon after, managers from the Tennessee plant came up to Windsor to describe their success and to answer more detailed questions.

By 1988 Windsor had embraced the idea, and by 1990 a network of Kodak plants around the country were engaged in the same process.

REALIZING THE VALUE OF EXPERIENCE

Even though quality circles fumbled at Windsor in the early 1980s—as they did at many American companies—the process of starting them up did produce two gains:

- Workers were trained in a valuable skill—the use of statistical controls. They now regularly use statistical methods to identify a process that is moving "out of control" and to search logically for cause and effect and solutions.

- Workers were exposed to new ways of working together in teams and to brainstorming together to solve problems.

The ultimate benefit was that employees were encouraged to become involved. Their solutions to problems often proved to be far less costly than what managers and engineers were likely to have recommended in the past. Small, incremental, continuous improvements and solutions to problems emerge from the workers' own experiences.

For example, workers familiar with operating a machine may know how to modify it to achieve newly required tighter tolerances, or how to cut down waste generated by the machine in the production process.

By contrast, the typical engineer's or manager's "answer" is, "Let's junk this machine and buy the new one now on the market."

The enlightened managers at Kodak Windsor now agree that full-scale introduction of new equipment and new technology is rarely the only method to get major gains in quality and productivity. Major changes in technology are costly to implement and expensive in terms of earnings. The new installations usually need long lead times before they have any major positive effects.

Instead of tossing out the old, Kodak now finds itself reaping a windfall of new ideas from experienced workers, many of whom now have an opportunity to suggest and implement solutions they had thought of years earlier.

Previously, many of these workers didn't think they could get their ideas through the corporate bureaucracy, or didn't believe that management cared about savings as small as a few square feet on each pass of hundreds of feet of material. Now they know managers welcome all ideas.

New workers quickly get caught up in the spirit of improvement and change. A newly hired worker operating a relatively simple piece of equipment for a few weeks observed something wasteful about the long-standard technique used to wrap wide rolls of sensitized paper with plastic wrap. He suggested that if the roller he used turned in the opposite direction, less plastic would be used for each wrap.

His supervisor brought in an engineer to see if the change was feasible. It was. That simple change now saves Kodak Windsor a little plastic wrap on each roll, and a great deal of wrap waste at the end of each year.

A few days after the roller was reversed, a division manager—three layers of supervision above the shop floor—ran into the worker who made the suggestion in an elevator and complimented him on the idea. The surprised and delighted worker blurted out, "I didn't think you even knew who I was."

A materials-handling manager now encourages operators who will be using equipment to visit suppliers, to try out different models and report on which ones they think are best and why.

Kodak, like many companies, long suffered from complaints by floor operators that the company spent a lot of money on "junk" that didn't work. Not anymore. Involvement brings commitment.

Management's decision about which equipment to buy might not necessarily turn out to be different as a result of input received from operators. But the fact that employees are actively involved in the decision-making process does have a big positive impact on the effective introduction of new equipment into the production cycle.

Managers now acknowledge that even the best

technical solution is doomed to fail if it's not supported by the people who have to work with the new equipment or new system every day. Even a poor technical solution that has operator support is likely to outproduce the latest technological wonder. Involving employees in making equipment decisions commits them to making the equipment perform.

Experience in working on teams within departments, between departments and even between plants and divisions now often leads to solutions to common problems, replacing the more typical finger-pointing and blame-laying that often hampers such efforts.

A case in point: A Windsor fork-lift operator expressed concern about the amount of paper wasted each time a rail-car load of photographic paper stock from Rochester, New York, was unloaded at the Colorado plant. He initiated a team analysis to identify what caused most of the torn paper. It turned out that the loading crew in Rochester strives to pack in the maximum load. But the way they accomplished that resulted in sizable damage to the rolls as the fork-lift operator in Windsor struggled to free the first one.

Before continuous improvement was on everyone's mind, nobody told the Rochester shipping crew about the problem at the receiving end. Now, by working together, employee teams at Rochester and Windsor figured out a new way to maximize the load on the rail car while eliminating the waste at the end of the line.

Three years before, the Windsor fork-lift operator had suggested something like that but nothing came of it. Now the solution to a problem may not even be eligible for a suggestion reward, because it came out of a team exercise. But he says he doesn't care. He knows it was his idea. He's glad the team finally got somebody to listen so the guys in Rochester changed the way they handled the loading process.

REVAMPING THE COMPANY SUGGESTION SYSTEM

Kodak has had a formal corporate suggestion system since 1898—the oldest one on record in the US. Over that time it has paid employees more than $40 million for more than 800,000 adopted suggestions. Cash awards range up to $50,000. In 1989, Kodak paid out $4.3 million in awards for suggestions that saved the company $22 million. By any objective standard, Kodak's suggestion system is a success.

But in the face of the swarm of suggestions and solutions that have resulted from recent efforts at Windsor and elsewhere to bring about continuous improvement, the traditional suggestion plan now seems to have limitations.

Many employees, and even some managers, consider the suggestion system to be excessively bureaucratic and slow to respond. An idea has to be written down and documented. It is then assigned to someone to investigate. The investigator's report is reviewed and signed by a manager, who then sends it along to a review committee. If the suggestion is finally approved, it goes back to another manager to be implemented. A suggestion usually takes at least four months to work its way through this path—and could take a year.

Moreover, employees are cautioned that "if the subject [of a suggestion] is related to your job responsibilities, you may not be eligible for an award." This restriction is in radical opposition to the whole idea of continuous-improvement programs. It probably dates from an assumption by designers of the original plan that supervisors and professionals would be the chief contributors of suggestions and they shouldn't be rewarded for making recommendations that were really a responsibility of the jobs they held.

The Kodak Corporate Suggestion Office, in response to the perceived shortcomings of the traditional plan, has been revising it. It now encourages supervisors throughout the company to experiment with tailor-made, small, but timely reward systems for individuals who suggest incremental improvements within their own areas of work. *Example:* An employee gets a silver dollar certificate for submitting an idea and $25 if the idea is implemented. The author of the idea is supposed to be able to implement it with minimal supervision if it is approved.

The workers at Windsor have gone far beyond this, however. In the lively climate of improvisation that now thrives there, they have devised their own idea-generating programs—and their own rewards for implemented improvements.

The monetary value of the rewards devised by the employees themselves is negligible compared with what they could potentially receive from the traditional corporate suggestion program. Nevertheless, the continuous-improvement programs have spurred a tenfold increase in the number of suggestions implemented.

In 1986, for instance, the 700 employees in the Wide Roll Manufacturing division at Kodak Windsor, which makes photographic paper stock and coats it, made a grand total of fewer than 60 suggestions through the corporate system. In 1989, the same workers made more than 3,000 implemented suggestions via the division's continuous-improvement program.

The new program at Windsor's Wide Roll division was not simply an overhaul of Kodak's vaunted company-wide suggestion system. It got its start in 1986, when a division manager attended a seminar at which he heard about a continuous-improvement program at an insurance company. He asked Jim Cole, then a manager in the division, to oversee a Wide Roll team effort to design their own plan.

Cole, working with seven production operators and mechanics in the division, came up with an initial plan and rewards—tokens worth a certain number of points that could be used in the company store to buy logo-imprinted clothing and other products. The ultimate reward for an individual who collected enough points: A day off. The day-off reward came right from the employees, Cole admits. No manager would have thought that up.

The team designed its own suggestion form. When the program began stimulating such an unexpected avalanche of ideas, the team revised the reward scale.

Initially, all ideas went directly to department managers. But the managers were soon so overloaded with suggestions that they turned them over for screening by first-line supervisors. These supervisors review ideas for general viability but have no power to reject or accept an idea on their own. At the time the department head gives a go-ahead to a suggestion, he/she also sets the point reward and makes sure the employees get the help they need to implement the idea.

Some suggested improvements are minor—moving paper-towel rolls in a laboratory or pencil sharpeners in offices so that they are more accessible—but quite a few are major improvements. A production operator figured out a way to avoid a long-standing problem in balancing air pressures outside and inside an enclosed processing device so that dirt is now less likely to sweep into the machine, contaminating a whole run of paper. The operator had actually thought of the solution to the problem some time before but was frustrated in finding a way to get it implemented until the new continuous-improvement program came along.

Improvisation and initiative provide the energy for Kodak Windsor's continuous-improvement effort. The 400-person finishing department for X-ray film, for instance, now thinks of itself as a silver mine, uncovering "silver nuggets" each time it comes up with a new way to eliminate waste—silver being a substantial component of the coating on photographic film or paper. The department's employees "own" the silver mine in which they work and regularly "declare a dividend" based on savings in waste achieved during that period.

Managers at Kodak Windsor have learned, moreover, how to manage the generation and implementation of suggestions so that individuals and teams don't go off on their own and do something that might create a safety or quality problem. The chief tool is training, training and more training, so that employees expand their understanding of how the whole system in which they work is interconnected and mutually responsive.

KEEPING TRACK OF SUCCESS

Managers also steer improvement and problem-solving efforts in directions most important to overall performance. At every level, managers analyze and weigh the specific criteria for success of that operation—cost reduction, quality improvement, delivery performance to customers, quality of work life, etc. In highly price-competitive lines of business, for example, managers make it clear that 90 percent of the continuous-improvement effort should go into reducing costs. In areas where maintaining market share depends more on keeping up and improving quality, perhaps only 60 percent of the effort may be directed to cost-cutting.

These weightings create what Kodak calls a management matrix—a balance of priorities for divisions, departments and, finally, individuals. Managers also negotiate these priority matrices between "suppliers" and "customers" within the company itself.

The key to success is to achieve direction without bureaucracy, forms, interminable meetings and top-down orders and decisions. That means using every implemented suggestion as a way of changing the culture of the operating unit so that the exchange of ideas becomes natural. Ideas then start to flow easily and casually and don't have to be flogged out of employees by the insistent demands of managers.

The Windsor philosophy has also affected the way cash bonuses are handled. The company-wide Kodak bonus system is designed to encourage better personal performance. The formulas used to determine awards are often complex and obscure, however, and many workers see little direct connection between the size of their bonuses and the specific efforts they make to improve performance.

At Windsor, however, a middle-level manager can run a small, easy-to-understand "bonus" system from his desk drawer. Like every other manager at Windsor, he includes a modest figure in his annual budget for informal rewards. These he distributes at his own discretion—on the spot—to people working for him who make a special contribution. The rewards range from wooden tokens (worth an ice cream at the company cafeteria) to dinner vouchers for employee and spouse at a local restaurant, including enough for a baby sitter.

Tracking results is critical for any continuous-improvement program. Windsor employees have found a variety of creative ways to keep track of their success in meeting objectives.

On a big wall inside the sensitizing complex in Windsor, for instance, employees have painted a brilliant mural of four snowcapped mountains in the foreground and a cone-shaped mountain in the distance that looks very much like Mount Fuji—a reminder of the company's chief worldwide competitor. Each of the four mountains is a "customer" of the sensitizing unit—other parts of the Windsor plant that receive the division's output of emulsion-clad film or paper stock to finish and package for end users.

Four figures of mountain climbers cling to the slopes of each of the four mountains on the mural—representing the four departments in the sensitizing division. As each department improves its performance in accordance with the priorities set in the matrix, employees move the climbers farther up the slope of the mountain. Anyone in the plant can see where each department stands and what progress it is making. When a climber reaches a peak—meeting the top performance standard—it's time for a party.

All of these reforms and imaginative retoolings of Kodak's original suggestion system—already known to be one of the best in business—are aimed at one thing: Unlocking the treasure trove of employee knowledge.

Kodak managers at Windsor now give warm praise to "the folks on the floor—the largest untapped resource we have." Production people, mechanics, the people servicing the process, know a lot about it. They have become an amazing source of new ideas now that they are confident Kodak really means business about going after them and getting those ideas.

The whole effort toward continuous improvement now permeates Kodak Windsor so thoroughly that in time, the phrase itself appeared on that quintessential tool of traditional management—the annual performance appraisal form. Individuals who have long been evaluated chiefly on their productivity, knowledge of the job and record of absenteeism are now also ranked on their "ability to work as a team member" and their "contribution to continuous improvement."

SEVEN LESSONS FROM KODAK

1. If the company is too large or too widely scattered geographically to initiate a continuous-improvement program throughout, consider using an outlying operation as a proving ground. It's often possible to get more successful momentum with a smaller group. There are only 2,500 employees at Kodak Windsor, compared with 43,000 at its Rochester, New York, headquarters, for instance.

2. If a continuous-improvement program initiated in a department, division, plant or office is successful, don't immediately attempt to "export" the same program to every part of the company. Other units may come up with different but equally good ideas that better reflect the rewards that motivate workers in that operation.

3. Stay alert for continuous-improvement ideas that are being tried out in other parts of the company or in other companies. Seminars and books are good ways to discover ideas. But "benchmark" these techniques before trying to adopt them. Give employees and managers opportunities to talk with other employees and managers in units (within the company or in other companies) where continuous improvement is successful so they can see in practical terms what is being done and how it affects the quality of work life.

4. Make managers responsible for setting priorities in the areas in which improvements are most crucial for the company's competitive success. Be sure they communicate those priorities clearly to the workers they supervise. Setting these priorities does not mean rejecting other worthwhile and useful ideas because they don't fall into line, however. Managers should work together with employees to set explicit improvement goals in these priority areas. Encourage workers with a common

interest in positive results to come up with a reward system on their own that monitors achievement and stimulates their initiative.

5. Examine the company's traditional corporate suggestion and bonus systems to see where they complement and strengthen continuous-improvement efforts and where they divert such efforts or are ineffectual. Survey employees at all levels on their understanding of how the suggestion, bonus and other incentive systems work and for their suggestions on improving the systems. Be prepared to make major changes.

6. Add "contribution to continuous improvement" and "ability to work on a team" as factors in annual employee performance appraisals.

7. Let managers add a budget line for small, on-the-spot rewards for special performance that they can give to individuals who report to them. These spontaneous rewards should be in addition to more formal reward systems set up for continuous improvements.